TABLE OF C

1. ABOUT THIS BOOK: 2019 PREFACE

When I introduced *Issa's Best: A Translator's Selection of Master Haiku* (2012), I described it as a book twenty-six years in the making—which means that now, in 2019, thirty-three years of studying, translating, and loving Issa have gone into it.

For that book I chose from among the haiku in my online archive (ten thousand of them) a bit over ten percent that, in my opinion, stand out as the best ever written by prolific Issa. Many readers told me that they liked the collection and thanked me for putting it together. I was happy.

Earlier this year, a recipient of the randomized Daily Issa feed on Yahoo Groups asked if I might also consider adding to the book the original Japanese versions, their romanized transliterations, and some critical commentary—where such comments might lead to a deeper appreciation and understanding.

I said, "Why not?"—and got to work.

I hope that this expanded version of *Issa's Best* helps readers come to know even more intimately this insightful, sensitive, big-hearted, deeply spiritual and forever inspiring, world-class poet. Kobayashi Issa lived, dreamed, and created in

A Taste of Issa

Haiku

By Kobayashi Issa

English translation by David G. Lanoue

HaikuGuy.com
New Orleans, Louisiana, USA

ISBN-13: 978-1-7333016-1-9

The cover image is a detail of an undated self-portrait by Issa that includes the poem,

ひいき目に見てさへ寒いそぶりかな
hiiki me ni mite sae samui soburi kana

even to my
biased eyes...
I look cold!

A Taste of Issa

Haiku

Japan's early modern Edo period.

Now, he belongs to the ages.

2. 2012 PREFACE (WITH SOME ADDITIONS)

In 1986 I began studying Japanese for the sole purpose of reading the haiku of Kobayashi Issa in its original form. By 1988 I had learned enough Japanese to begin translating Issa's one-breath poems to English. My first book, *Issa: Cup-of-Tea Poems; Selected Haiku of Kobayashi Issa*, came out in 1992; in it, I presented 450 haiku of Issa in seasonal order. In the year 2000 I launched my *Haiku of Kobayashi Issa* website, a searchable archive that at that time contained a database of 500 poems. Today that database has reached 10,000—a little less than half of Issa's total output.

Issa: Cup-of-Tea Poems is now out of print, and though in 2009 I brought out a selection of 162 of his haiku in a bilingual English-Hindi edition published in India (*The Distant Mountain: The Life and Haiku of Kobayashi Issa*), for a long time I have been contemplating the possibility of putting together a more substantial collection of Issa's haiku. While I intend to continue to offer all of the 10,000 poems that I have translated free to the world on the Internet, the present book is a guided tour through the work of Issa, gathering together in one text approximately 1,200 of what I consider to be the master poet's most effective and evocative verses.

The haiku presented in this book are divided into six

sections. The first is "New Year's/Beginning of Spring." In the old Japanese calendar, New Year's Day was considered the first day of spring. It took place well over a month after our modern, Western New Year's Day. For Japanese haiku poets of the Edo period, New Year's Day, including the weeks following it—filled with sundry celebrations and rituals—was considered a season on its own. The next four sections—"Spring," "Summer," "Autumn" and "Winter"—contain haiku pertaining to these respective seasons. The final section offers a handful of Issa's haiku without seasonal references and, in one case, a haiku of mixed seasons that evokes both "blossoms" (associated with spring) and "moon" (associated with autumn). In this interesting poem, Issa transcends any single point in the cycle of the year to reflect, metaphorically, on his whole life and on life itself. In this section we also find some haiku about elements and animals that appear all year round, thus lacking any specific seasonal affiliation.

3. ABOUT ISSA

The poet we know today as Issa was born on the fifth day of Fifth Month of 1763 (June 15 on the Western calendar) in Kashiwabara, a small village in the highlands of Shinano Province, today's Nagano Prefecture. His family name was Kobayashi; his given name, Yatarō. His father was a well-to-do farmer who owned enough land that the family's economic status, in the context of time and place, was closer to middle class than peasant. Yatarō's mother must have been warm and loving; he never recovered emotionally from her dying when he was three years old. He writes about her 47 years later, at age fifty:

> my dead mother—
> every time I see the ocean
> every time...

His mother's replacement in the household, Satsu, soon gave birth to a son of her own, and treated young Yatarō cruelly, according to the latter's journal accounts, years later. For maternal love, he turned to his grandmother, but her death in 1776, when he was fourteen, was a second heart-crushing loss. The hostility directed at him by his stepmother Satsu disrupted domestic tranquility so much, Yatarō was sent away by his father to Edo, today's Tokyo, a year later. He was fifteen years old in the Japanese age-reckoning system, according to which a person gains a year of age with each New Year's Day after birth. By Western standards, he was only thirteen. The historical record is silent on what type of servile or manual labor he found in Edo.

He joined the hordes of migrant workers from outlying provinces who swarmed every year into Edo to provide that city with a good portion of its labor force, surfacing in 1787 as a member of a haiku school led by Chikua: the Nirokuan. He eventually adopted the penname of Issa, "One Tea" or, more idiomatically, "Cup-of-Tea." The emotionally wounded, unwanted stepchild of the mountains had found poetry, or perhaps poetry had found him. Either way, he decided to dedicate his life to the way of haiku or, as it was called in Issa's day, *haikai*.

At age 29, inspired by the example set by the first great haiku master, Matsuo Bashō (1644-94), Issa took to the road on the first of a series of haiku-writing journeys. He describes himself in this period: "Rambling to the west, wandering to the east, there is a madman who never stays in one place. In the morning, he eats breakfast in Kazusa; by evening, he finds lodging in Musashi. Helpless as a white wave, apt to vanish like a bubble in froth—he is named Priest Issa."

"Priest Issa" visited his home village of Kashiwabara in Third Month of 1801, in time to find his father sick and dying. He tended to his father and vowed to him that he would stop wandering and return to live in the family homestead. According to Issa's poetic diary that covers this episode, *The Journal of My Father's Last Days* (*Chichi no Shūen Nikki* 父の 終焉日記), stepmother Satsu and half brother Senroku rejected the dying wish of their husband and father, respectively, and refused to allow Issa's return, thus setting off a long and bitter legal struggle. Finally, in autumn of 1813, the village headman decided that the Kobayashi house would be partitioned and that Issa would be permitted to live in one side of it. With great joy the poet moved in after 36 years of exile, and, two years later, married a local woman, Kiku. They proceeded to start a family of their own.

Much ink has been spilled about the ensuing tragedies that marred Issa's homecoming joy: four of his children dying, one by one, from diseases such as smallpox and, in one case, accidental suffocation. Especially devastating to the poet was the death of little Sato, his precious daughter, in 1819—a loss recounted in his journal *My Spring* (*Oraga haru*). Her death inspired one of his most poignant and famous verses:

> this world
> is a dewdrop world
> yes... but...

His wife Kiku's death in 1823 was another awful blow, but critics of Issa should beware of letting these family tragedies become the dominant theme when writing about him and his poetry. While he certainly mourns in his haiku, in times of mourning, he also laughs in times of laughter, gasps in moments of surprise...and so on. From his mid-twenties on, he was a prolific, dedicated writer committed to discovering the meaning of all of his moods—happy, sad, silly, reflective—in haiku. The image of him as a poet weighed down by "the sorrow of life" (to translate the title of one Japanese book about him) is grossly inaccurate.

Just as significant as the sorrows of this period of his maturity is the fact that his reputation as a teacher of haiku was spreading far and wide. Issa enjoyed great celebrity in his home province of Shinano, as well as in Edo and surrounding areas, where he visited from time to time. The period 1812 to 1824 represents the peak years of his poetry, but what kind of poetry was it?

He is known for four characteristics for which he was unrivaled by the other great figures of haiku tradition. The first is his warm, loving connection with living things, especially animals but also including humans and plants. As a Buddhist artist brimming with compassion and respect for his fellow beings, however small, Issa likes to address his nonhuman colleagues directly—a thing that prompts many critics to label him as a poet of "personification" or "anthropomorphism."

does the red dawn
delight you
snail?

In light of his Buddhist faith, however, he is not projecting "human" attributes on the snail—a fellow traveler on the road of existence. For Issa, even a snail can have a poet's heart that delights in the colors of the morning sky.

A second characteristic is his comedy. Issa perceives the ironic, the off-kilter and the absurd—and is prone to express such perceptions with the perfect timing of a master joke teller in his one-breath poetry. However, his comic approach should not be misunderstood as flippant or intellectually shallow. He rejects the tragic gesture of clinging to things, people, even to his own happiness—all of which must, inevitably, fade away. Instead, he approaches the universe with the comic gesture of not grasping: of letting go and surrendering to it with good humor.

the year's first rain—
my grass roof's
first leak

Though he often mentions his own poverty, referring to his home as a hermit's hut or a "Trash House" (*kuzuya* 屑家), Issa accepts his situation, and all the rain that comes leaking in on New Year's Day. Some might worry or even weep in such circumstances; Issa chooses acceptance...and laughter.

A third characteristic of Issa is how he transforms the personal into art. He doesn't hesitate to tell the story of his life in his haiku. I've already mentioned his poems of mourning for lost loved ones that some readers and critics tend to overemphasize. His complete works include verses that relate all sorts of situations and moods in highly personal, intimately autobiographical statements.

> in hazy night
> stepping into water...
> losing my way

It was a hazy night of spring in 1795. In the uncertain, dreamlike light, Issa stepped off a path into water. We know from his travel journal that he was attempting to visit, that night, a friend and Buddhist priest, Sarai, who, he discovered, had been dead for several years. After being told of his friend's death, Issa begged Sarai's replacement at the temple for a night's stay, but was refused. He had come over 300 *ri* (1,178 kilometers), "without a soul to lean on, going over the fields and the yards..." In light of this biographical context, the phrase in the haiku, "losing my way," has deep, troubling resonance.

A fourth characteristic at which Issa surpasses all competition among masters of haiku is his propensity for defending the

15

underdog, or at times, the under-frog.

> scrawny frog, hang tough!
> Issa
> is here

Issa's vision is democratic and often iconoclastic. His verses are filled with images of figures of authority in silly postures (a high priest of a temple pooping in a field) and reflections on the meaninglessness of human hierarchy and social class (a war lord or "daimyō" forced to dismount from his horse because of the higher power of...cherry blossoms!). This is why Issa is so loved by Japanese people. Bashō and Buson are perceived as revered masters of haiku sitting on high seats of honor; Issa stands shoulder-to-shoulder with common folk, shunning and lampooning authority and pretense.

> looks like the boss
> in the seat of honor...
> croaking frog

As far as his biography goes, there are only a few more key facts that the reader should know. In 1824, at age 62, he married for a second time, briefly, but divorced within three months. In 1826, he married his third wife, Yao. In 1827, his house burned down in a fire that swept through Kashiwabara village. He and his wife moved into a small, musty grain barn—a structure that still stands today—where he died on the nineteenth day of Eleventh Month of the Tenth Year of the Bunsei Era, the equivalent Western date being January 5, 1828.

In the mid-19th century, in 1851, Issa's poetic diary of 1819, *Oraga haru*, was published with two postscripts that reveal how he was perceived by his countrymen 24 years after his death. In the first postscript, Seian Saiba mentions his humor but hastens to add that "sarcasm is not the main object of this priest; his writing also contains loneliness, laughter, and sadness; and it expresses human feeling, worldly conditions, and transience." The author of the second postscript, Hyōkai Shisanjin, agrees: "Though it has a bit of jest in it, [Issa's poetry] visits well the way of Buddhism... boldly not loathing the dust of this world and filled with human feeling." Half-hidden within his haiku jokes are profound and sincere Buddhist lessons about worldly conditions and the transience of things. This is how the generation after him viewed his poetry.

In the more secular 20th century, the spiritual aspect of Issa's writing gradually faded from the attention of critics, who chose instead to dwell on biographical details, especially those details, as I have mentioned, having to do with suffering and loss. There were exceptions, of course: in 1969 Murata Shōcho published a study of Issa in connection to Pure Land Buddhism, *Haikai-ji Issa no geijutsu* 俳諧寺一茶の

17

藝術 ("The Art of Haiku Temple Issa"), a title derived from the verse:

> new spring
> Yatarō is reborn...
> into Haiku Temple

Yatarō, we remember, was Issa's given name. This poem celebrates his "rebirth" as a poet-priest, serving in the "temple" of haiku. My own books, *Pure Land Haiku: The Art of Priest Issa* (2004), *Issa and the Meaning of Animals* (2014), and *Issa and Being Human* (2017) continue in the tradition of Seian Saiba, Hyōkai Shisanjin, and Murata Shōcho in asserting that Issa is a spiritual poet for whom Buddhism and haiku are one thing.

Today, Issa is a world treasure. Though his popularity in Japan persists, with new books about him appearing every year, he is becoming just as recognized and admired in other countries, as more and more translations, like the present one, are published. He is a poet who speaks to our common humanity in a way that is so honest, so contemporary, his verses might have been written this morning. Bashō is the most revered of the haiku poets of Old Japan, but Issa is the most loved.

4. NEW YEAR'S/SPRING BEGINS

1795

元日やさらに旅宿とおもほへず
ganjitsu ya sara ni ryoshuku to omohoezu

New Year's Day—
that I'm still on this journey
unbelievable

This haiku is the lead poem in Issa's 1795 travel journal, *Saigoku kikō* 西国紀行 ("Western Provinces Travelogue"); *Issa zenshū* 一茶全集 [henceforth *IZ*] (Nagano: Shinano Mainichi Shimbunsha, 1976-79) 5.35. *Sara ni* さらに signifies "once more" or "over again." In this situation, it means, "still." Issa is still on his great journey—a fact that seems, suddenly, incredible to him.

1809

元日や我のみならぬ巣なし鳥
ganjitsu ya ware nominaranu su nashi tori

on New Year's Day
I have company
bird without a nest

A fire swept through Edo (old Tokyo) that New Year's Day,

19

destroying Issa's house. When he wrote this haiku he was literally homeless.

1810

家なしも江戸の元日したりけり
ie nashi mo edo no ganjitsu shitari keri

homeless, too
seeing in the new year
in Edo

In 1810 Issa was trying hard to resolve the inheritance dispute with his stepmother, who was blocking his return to the family house in his native village of Kashiwabara. He spent the auspicious day meant for family and togetherness in the big city of Edo—by himself.

1814

かれらにも元日させん鳩すずめ
karera ni mo ganjitsu-sasen hato suzume

for them too
a New Year's feast...
pigeons, sparrows

1817

元日をするや揃ふて小田の雁

ganjitsu wo suru ya soroute oda no kari

celebrating New Year's
en masse...
rice field geese

1821

元日も立のままなる屑家哉

ganjitsu mo tatsu no mama naru kuzuya kana

on New Year's Day, too
standing "as is"...
trashy house

1821

元日やどちらむいても花の娑婆

ganjitsu ya dochira muite mo hana no shaba

on New Year's Day
everywhere, a corrupt world's
blossoms

The word *shaba* 娑婆 refers to the Buddhist notion of a fallen age, the "Latter Days of Dharma." In Pure Land Buddhist belief, the present age of *mappō* 末法 is the third and worst of three ages that followed the historical Buddha's achievement of nirvana. First came the age of Right Dharma (*shōbō* 正法) during which Buddhist teaching, practice, and enlightenment all existed. According to Shinran, this golden age lasted five hundred years. Next came a millennium of Imitative Dharma (*zōbō* 象法), when only teaching and practice were possible, not enlightenment. The present, third age of *mappō*, the Latter Days of Dharma, comprises a ten thousand year period of corruption in which only Buddhist teaching survives; practice and enlightenment are unattainable through ego-corrupted self-power (*jiriki* 自力). In our depraved age, Shinran insists, only the Other Power (*tariki* 他力) of Amida Buddha can bring about enlightenment.

1824

世の中をゆり直すらん日の始
yo no naka wo yuri naosuran hi no hajime

maybe this quake
will put the world right...
year's first day

This is the first haiku of the Seventh Year of the Bunsei Era, which has a Western equivalent of January 31, 1824. According to Issa's diary, there was an earthquake that day in the afternoon (3:00-5:00 p.m.); *IZ* 4.465. Makoto Ueda believes that Issa is referring to his own life in this haiku, his longing to change course in his "private world"; *Dew on the Grass: The Life and Poetry of Kobayashi Issa* (Leiden/Boston: Brill, 2004) 152. Another way of reading the haiku is to see it as a more universal statement. In this fallen age of *mappō* the world needs healing. Perhaps a good shake, Issa hopes, will set things right.

1825
元日や闇いうちから猫の恋
ganjitsu ya kurai uchi kara neko no koi

New Year's Day—
in the dark before dawn
the lover cat

year unknown
元日の日向ぼこする屑家かな
ganjitsu no hinata bokosuru kuzuya kana

basking
in the New Year's sun...
my trashy hut

year unknown

元日や上々吉の浅黄空

ganjitsu ya jōjōkichi no asagi-zora

on New Year's Day
lucky! lucky!
a pale blue sky

year unknown

昼頃に元日になる庵かな

hiru-goro ni ganjitsu ni naru iori kana

around noon
New Year's Day begins...
little hut

Issa flaunts his laziness, even on this most auspicious day of the year.

1808

あら玉のとし立かへる虱哉

aratama no toshi tachikaeru shirami kana

a shiny-new year
has come again...
for my lice

The first word in this haiku, *aratama* あら玉, denotes an

unpolished gem. The expression *aratama no* is often used to describe a year, a month, a day, a season, and so on; *Kogo dai jiten* 古語大辞典 [henceforth *KGJ*] (Shogakukan 1983) 79.

1822

年立やもとの愚が又愚にかへる
toshi tatsu ya moto no gu ga mata gu ni kaeru

a new year—
the same nonsense
piled on nonsense

1806

又ことし娑婆塞ぞよ草の家
mata kotoshi shaba-fusage zo yo kusa no ie

another year
just taking up space...
thatched hut

1821

ことしから手左り笠に小風呂敷
kotoshi kara te hidari kasa ni ko-buroshiki

from this year on
in my left hand, umbrella-hat
in the right, knapsack

In Issa's day there was no knapsack per se. A *furoshiki* 風呂敷 (cloth in which items could be wrapped and carried) fulfilled this function. Issa is carrying his umbrella-hat in his left hand, and "hand baggage" in his right. The meaning of this New Year's poem, then, is that he has re-committed himself to a life of poetic wandering.

1797

正月の子供に成て見たき哉
shōgatsu no kodomo ni natte mitaki kana

becoming a child
on New Year's Day...
I wish!

This is the starting verse of a 36-verse *kasen* renku made by Issa and the most prominent poet of Matsuyama City (where he was visiting), Kurita Chodō. Issa's wish to become a child again isn't completely absurd, for it is his mission as a haiku poet to see the world with open, nonjudgmental, childlike eyes. Too many adults, in their daily rush, hurry past nature's treasures without paying attention to them, without really seeing them. This year, Issa vows to do otherwise.

1804

正月やよ所に咲ても梅の花
shōgatsu ya yoso ni saite mo ume no hana

First Month—
the plum trees blooming
elsewhere

1808

古羽織長の正月も過にけり
furu haori naga no shōgatsu mo sugi ni keri

my old coat—
a long First Month
creeps by

Or: "the old coat." Issa doesn't specify that it is his, but this might be inferred. Even though the First Month coincides with the beginning of spring, it's still cold enough for Issa to wear his Japanese coat (*haori* 羽織).

1813

正月や梅のかはりの大吹雪
shōgatsu ya ume no kawari no ōfubuki

First Month—
instead of plum blossoms
a blizzard

27

1814

正月や辻の仏も赤頭巾
shōgatsu ya tsuji no hotoke mo aka zukin

First Month—
on the crossroads Buddha
a red skullcap

1818

正月やえたの玄関も梅の花
shōgatsu ya eta no genkan mo ume no hana

First Month—
even at the outcaste's porch
plum blossoms

This haiku refers to the outcastes (*eta* えた). In Issa's time, they performed "unclean" jobs such as disposing of dead animals, working with leather, and executing criminals. They were subject to discrimination and racial prejudice, and yet, Issa notes, the plum blossoms bloom for them, too.

1821

正月の二ッもなまけ始かな
shōgatsu no futatsu mo namake hajime kana

First Month, second day
the laziness
begins

year unknown

正月や現金酒の通ひ帳

shōgatsu ya genkin sake no kayoichō

First Month—
recording the cash spent
on sake

At the end of the year debts were supposed to be settled.
However, as my Japanese advisor Shinji Ogawa points out,
Issa "obviously has not paid his last year's debt," which
means he needs to pay cash for his New Year's sake.

year unknown

猫塚に正月させるごまめ哉

neko tsuka ni shōgatsu saseru gomame kana

on the cat's grave
in First Month...
dried sardines

1810

老が身の値ぶみをさるるけさの春

oi ga mi no nebumi wo saruru kesa no haru

taking stock
of this old body...
spring's first dawn

Jean Cholley notes that Issa wrote this haiku at the beginning of his 48th year, which was considered an advanced age at the time; *En village de miséreux: Choix de poèmes de Kobayashi Issa* (Paris: Gallimard, 1996) 238.

1817

影ぼしもまめ息災でけさの春
kageboshi mo mame sokusai de kesa no haru

> my shadow too
> in good health...
> dawn of spring

Sokusai 息災 is a word with special resonance for Buddhists, signifying a sense of tranquility in the knowledge that the merits of Buddhism can overcome the misfortunes of this world; *KDJ* 927.

1818

這へ笑へ二ッになるぞけさからは
hae warae futatsu ni naru zo kesa kara wa

> crawl and laugh—
> from this morning on
> a two year old!

The child in question is Sato, who would die on the 21st day of Sixth Month, 1819. Though Issa wrote this haiku in Twelfth

Month 1818, he anticipates in it the coming New Year's Day of 1819, at which time Sato would turn two by traditional reckoning. By Western reckoning she was seven months' old that day.

1819

鶯のいな鳴やうも今朝の春
uguisu no i na naki yō mo kesa no haru

the nightingale's song
wonderfully strange…
spring's first dawn

1820

弥陀仏をたのみに明て今朝の春
mida butsu wo tanomi ni akete kesa no haru

in Amida Buddha
trusting…
spring's first dawn

year unknown
けさ春と掃まねしたりひとり坊
kesa haru to haku mane shitari hitori-bō

spring's first dawn—
the priest pretending
to sweep

Issa called himself "Priest Issa of the Temple of Haikai"
(*haikai* 俳諧 being what today we call haiku). It's possible
that the priest in this verse is Issa.

year unknown
ふしぎ也生れた家でけさの春
fushigi nari umareta ie de kesa no haru

amazing—
in the house I was born
spring's first morning

1795
乞食も護摩酢酌むらん今日の春
konjiki mo gomazu kumuran kyō no haru

even beggars toast
with sesame sake...
first of spring

Issa more exactly is saying, "Perhaps even beggars may toast..." In English, the "perhaps" and "may" weaken the poem, so I've left them out.

1819

あばら家や其身其まま明の春
abaraya ya sono mi sono mama ake no haru

my ramshackle hut—
just as it is...
spring begins

On New Year's Day, others diligently sweep and decorate their gates with pine-and-bamboo arrangements, but Issa's hermitage remains "just as it is." This attitude of *sono mama* 其まま, being "just as one is," is appropriate for the practice of Jōdoshinshū Buddhism. The sect founder, Shinran, urges that one not strive or calculate to attain enlightenment but, instead, simply accept Amida Buddha's liberating power just as he or she is: sinful and human.

1823

武士町やしんかんとして明の春
bushi machi ya shinkan to shite ake no haru

the samurai street
perfectly silent
spring's first dawn

1804

又士になりそこなうて花の春
mata tsuchi ni narisokonaute hana no haru

once again
I've managed not to die...
blossoming spring

1809

家なしの身に成て見る花の春
ie nashi no mi ni natte miru hana no haru

now with homeless eyes
I see it...
blossoming spring

In this haiku Issa alludes, once again, to the 1809 fire in Edo that burned down the place he was staying.

1813

すりこ木のやうな歯茎も花の春
surikogi no yōna haguki mo hana no haru

with gums for grinders
greeting the blossoming
spring

1821

門口や自然生なる松の春
kado-guchi ya jinen bae-naru matsu no haru

at my gate
wildly it grows...
spring pine

1822

引窓の一度にあくや江戸の春
hikimado no ichi do ni aku ya edo no haru

all the windows
slid wide open...
Edo's spring

1820

鶯のくる影ぼしも窓の春
uguisu no kuru kageboshi mo mado no haru

the nightingale comes
with his shadow...
spring window

1819

日出度さもちう位也おらが春
medetasa mo chū kurai nari oraga haru

my "Happy New Year!"
about average…
my spring

With deadpan humor Issa describes his joy of the New Year's season as "about average" (*chū kurai* ちう位). This famous haiku is the opening verse in Issa's 1819 haibun, *Oraga haru* おらが春 ("My Spring")—and the source of that work's title.

1807

はつ春やけぶり立るも世間むき
hatsu haru ya keburi tateru mo seken muki

spring begins—
I send up my smoke
like everyone else

1808

貧乏草愛たき春に逢にけり

bimbō-gusa medetaki haru ni ai ni keri

the wild daisies
are celebrating...
spring's first day

1821

初春のけ形りは我と雀かな

hatsu haru no kenari wa ware to suzume kana

we start the spring
in our everyday clothes...
me and the sparrow

1803

春立といふばかりでも草木哉

haru tatsu to iu bakari demo kusaki kana

"Spring begins"
just saying it...
green everywhere

1805

ちぐはぐの下駄から春は立にけり
chiguhagu no geta kara haru wa tachi ni keri

the offbeat clomping
of clogs...
must be spring!

year unknown

我国はけぶりも千代のためし哉
waga kuni wa keburi mo chiyo no tameshi kana

my province—
even the smoke
an ancient thing

1811

春立や夢に見てさへ小松原
haru tatsu ya yume ni mite sae ko matsu-bara

spring's begun—
I even dream about
the grove of young pines

1817

春立や牛にも馬にもふまれずに
haru tatsu ya ushi ni mo uma nimo fumarezu ni

a new spring—
neither cow nor horse
has trod on it

1818

春立や弥太郎改め一茶坊
haru tatsu ya yatarō aratame issa-bō

new spring
Yatarō dies, priest Issa
is born

Yatarō was Issa's given name. In this haiku he celebrates his "rebirth" as Issa, which literally means "One Tea" 一茶. Issa's life has metaphorical, universal significance in his haiku. Here, he appears as a pilgrim Everyman rejoicing in a new identity and new beginning. The fact that he gives himself the title of *bō* 坊 (Buddhist priest) indicates that for Issa the way of haiku will be a spiritual journey.

1821

春立や切口上の門雀
haru tatsu ya kirikōjō no kado suzume

spring begins—
the obligatory
sparrows at the gate

1823

春立や愚の上に又愚にかへる
haru tatsu ya gu no ue ni mata gu ni kaeru

spring begins—
more foolishness
for this fool

This first haiku of the year is preceded by a prose passage in which Issa, paraphrasing Bashō, comments on his own lack of talents. Makoto Ueda believes that Issa's self-mockery is really a subtle self-compliment. I agree; *Dew on the Grass* 144-45.

year unknown

はる立や門の雀もまめなかほ

haru tatsu ya kado no suzume mo mamena kao

spring begins—
sparrows at my gate
with healthy faces

1814

あつさりと春は来にけり浅黄空

assari to haru wa ki ni keri asagi-zora

spring comes simply
with a pale blue
sky

Students of Japanese might be surprised to see Issa's spelling of *assari* as あつさり instead of あっさり. In his day smaller hiragana were not required.

1803

首上て亀も待たる初日哉

kubi agete kame mo machitaru hatsu hi kana

stretching his neck
the turtle waits too...
the year's first day

1818

内中にてらてら鍬の初日哉

uchi-uchi ni tera-tera kuwa no hatsu hi kana

in the storehouse
the hoe glinting...
year's first dawn

1811

壁の穴や我初空もうつくしき

kabe no ana ya waga hatsuzora mo utsukushiki

hole in the wall
pretty
my year's first sky

1811

初空へさし出す獅子の首哉

hatsuzora e sashidasu shishi no kashira kana

to the year's first sky
the lion puppet
rears his head

Issa is referring to *shishimai* 獅子舞 "lion dance," a popular New Year's entertainment featuring lion puppets of various sizes.

1817

はつ空の祝儀や雪のちらちらと
hatsuzora no shūgi ya yuki no chira-chira to

the year's first sky
gives a gift...
snow flitting down

1817

初空の行留り也上総山
hatsuzora no yukidomari nari kazusa yama

the year's first sky
hits a dead end...
Kazusa mountains

Kazusa was a province in the Kantō area.

1819

西方のはつ空拝む法師哉
saihō no hatsu-zora ogamu hōshi kana

westward he prays
to the year's first sky...
priest

The priest faces west for a good reason: this is the direction of Amida Buddha's Pure Land.

1819
御盛りや草の庵ももりはじめ
osagari ya kusa no iori mo mori hajime

the year's first rain—
my grass roof's
first leak

Issa seems to complain about his leaky roof. Deep-down, is he proud of his ramshackle hut and the "just as I am" lifestyle that it represents?

year unknown
大原や恵方に出し杖の穴
ōhara ya ehō ni ideshi tsue no ana

big field—
my New Year's walk
follows holes made by canes

This haiku refers to the New Year's custom of visiting a shrine or temple located in a lucky direction.

1821

とぶ工夫猫のしてけり恵方棚
tobu kufū neko no shite keri ehōdana

the cat considers
jumping up...
New Year's offering shelf

The cat takes aim at the *ehōdana* 恵方棚, a New Year's shelf positioned so that people facing it would face an auspicious direction (determined by the location of a shrine where the Lucky Direction Goddess Toshitokujin was making her New Year's visit). The cat's less than pious motive seems to be to steal a food offering.

1821

呑連の常恵方也上かん屋
nomi-zure no jōehō nari jōkanya

for drinking buddies
the usual New Year's pilgrimage...
sake shop

1815

人の日や本堂いづる汗けぶり
hito no hi ya hondō izuru ase keburi

Mankind's Day—
from the main temple
the steam of bodies

This haiku has the headnote, "Mankind's Day, Main Temple." Mankind's Day (*hito no hi* 人の日) is the seventh day of First Month, at which time the seven herbs of health are boiled with rice gruel.

1820

梅咲や地獄の門も休み札
ume saku ya jigoku no kado mo yasumi satsu

plum blooming—
even hell's gate
CLOSED

1814

世の中はどんどと直るどんど哉
yo no naka wa don do to naoru dondo kana

this world of ours—
so fast the bonfires
burn out

This haiku refers to the "Little New Year," i.e. the day occurring on the year's first full moon: First Month, fifteenth day. At this time the New Year's decorations of pine-and-bamboo and sacred Shinto rope are burned. The New Year's bonfires quickly return to their original state, i.e. to nothingness—a Buddhist lesson in *mujō* 無常, the transience of all things.

1817

薮入や涙先立人の親
yabuiri ya namida sakidatsu hito no oya

homecoming servant—
tears precede everything
for the parents

After New Year's (on the sixteenth day of First Month), servants in the cities were given time off to return to their native villages and families.

1821

小松引人とて人のおがむ也
ko matsu hiku hito tote hito no ogamu nari

yanking up a little pine
he says
a prayer

Pulling up a young pine tree on the first day of the Year of

47

the Rat is a custom that originated in China. A more literal paraphrase of this haiku would be, "Even though he is a man yanking up a little pine, he is also a praying man." Issa alludes to the Buddhist precept against taking life—in this case, that of a plant which, in Issa's opinion (expressed in one of his journals) might one day become a Buddha.

1818

犬の子やかくれんぼする門の松
inu no ko ya kakurenbo suru kado no matsu

the puppy plays
hide-and-seek...
New Year's pine

The puppy is hiding behind the pine-and-bamboo New Year's decoration.

1814

福わらや雀が踊る鳶がまふ
fukuwara ya suzume ga odoru tobi ga mau

fresh straw for the garden!
a sparrow dances
a black kite wheels

In the New Year's season, new straw is spread in gardens in a purification ritual; *KDJ* 1433. The "black kite" in the scene (*tobi* 鳶) is a bird, not the paper kind.

1821

御年初を申し入れけり狐穴
o-nensho wo mōshi-ire keri kitsune ana

sending a "Happy
New Year!"
down the fox's hole

1824

むく起の小便ながら御慶哉
muku oki no shōben nagara gyokei kana

while taking
my morning piss...
"Happy New Year!"

1819

かくれ家や猫にも一ッ御年玉
kakurega ya neko ni mo hitotsu o-toshidama

secluded house—
even for the cat
a New Year's gift

1821

一番のとし玉ぞ其豆な顔

ichi ban no toshi-dama zo sono mamena kao

the best New Year's
present!
her pink cheeks

1821

とし玉の上にも猫のぐる寝哉

toshidama no ue ni mo neko no gurune kana

on top
of the New Year's gifts...
cat curled asleep

1824

年玉や懐の子も手々をして

toshi-dama ya futokoro no ko mo te-te wo shite

New Year's present—
the nursing baby reaches
with little hands

year unknown

いく廻り目だぞとし玉扇又もどる

iku meguri me da zo toshidama ōgi mata modoru

how many times
a New Year's gift?
the fan returns

1821

何のその上初夢もなく烏

nanno sono jō hatsu yume mo naku karasu

you've wrecked
my year's first dream!
cawing crow

1823

片乳を握りながらやはつ笑ひ

kata chichi wo nigiri nagara ya hatsu warai

while grasping
mama's breast...
the year's first laughter

1823

乞食やもらひながらのはつ笑ひ

kojiki ya morai nagara no hatsu warai

a beggar receives
alms, the year's first
laughter

year unknown

浴みして旅のしらみを罪始め

yuami shite tabi no shirami wo tsumi hajime

first hot bath—
for my journey's lice
first sin

Shinji Ogawa explains that Issa is punning in this haiku. The final phrase, *tsumi hajime* 罪始め not only denotes "first sin" but suggests that the poet is "pinching" the lice, after his bath.

1795

凧青葉を出つ入つ哉

ikanobori aoba wo idetsu iritsu kana

New Year's kite—
out of green leaves
then back in

1807

けふもけふも凧引かかる榎哉

kyō mo kyō mo tako hikkakaru enoki kana

today too, today too
the nettle tree snags
the kite

1807

猿引は猿に持せて凧

saru hiki wa saru ni motasete ikanobori

the trainer lets
his monkey hold it...
New Year's kite

1810

朔日や一文凧も江戸の空

tsuitachi ya ichi mon-dako mo edo no sora

New Year's Day—
a one-penny kite, too
in Edo's sky

The *mon* 文was the basic currency of Issa's time. It took the form of a coin with a hole in its middle so that it could be strung on a string. In Issa's day six *mon* could pay for a bowl of rice. Even though the kite would cost over twenty pennies in modern currency, I have kept it in my translation as a "one-penny kite," to emphasize its cheapness and the fact that only one small coin buys it.

1811
今様の凧上りけり乞食小屋
ima yō no tako agari keri kojiki goya

a trendy kite soars—
below
a beggar's hut

1822
すすけ紙まま子の凧としられけり
susuke-gami mamako no tako to shirare keri

made with sooty paper
the stepchild's kite
easy to spot

Issa was a stepchild—unloved, neglected, abused. Even at age sixty he remembers.

1822

凧の糸引とらまへて寝る子哉

tako no ito hikitoramaete neru ko kana

clinging to the kite's
string...
the sleeping child

1822

凧の尾を咥て引や鬼瓦

tako no o wo kuwaete hiku ya onigawara

catching the kite's tail
with his mouth...
gargoyle

1811

万歳や馬の尻へも一祝

manzai ya uma no shiri e mo hito iwai

begging actors—
even the horse's rump
gets a song

This haiku refers to begging actors who make their rounds
during the New Year's season performing a traditional style
of stand-up comedy.

1816

我国は猿も烏帽子をかぶりけり
waga kuni wa saru mo eboshi wo kaburi keri

in my province
even trained monkeys
wear noble hats

A satirical jab? Literally, Issa says that the monkey is wearing the courtly headgear of a nobleman. Dancing monkeys perform their tricks in the New Year's season.

1821

舞猿や餅いただきて子にくれる
mai saru ya mochi itadakite ko ni kureru

dancing monkey—
he gives his rice cake
to the child

1811

獅子舞や大口明て梅の花
shishimai ya ōkuchi akete ume no hana

the lion puppet
opens wide...
plum blossoms

1804

あらためて鶴もおりるか初わかな
aratamete tsuru mo oriru ka hatsu wakana

are you coming down
crane, to see?
picking herbs

Wakana わかな (young greens or herbs) are picked on the sixth day of First Month—a traditional New Year's observance.

1821

一引はたばこかすみやわかなつみ
hito hiki wa tabako kasumi ya wakana tsumi

for each one picked
a puff on the pipe...
herbs

5. SPRING

1807

鶯の東訛りも春辺哉
uguisu no azuma namari mo harube kana

the nightingale sings
with a country twang...
springtime

Issa is alluding to a Kasai accent. A subway stop in Greater Tokyo today, in Issa's time Kasai was a farming village east of Edo.

1811

月さして一文橋の春辺哉
tsuki sashite ichi mon hashi no harube kana

moon shining
on a one-penny bridge...
springtime

1812

辻だんぎちんぷんかんも長閑哉
tsuji dangi chinpunkan mo nodoka kana

a crossroads sermon
gibberish
spring peace

1819

長閑さや浅間のけぶり昼の月
nodokasa ya asama no keburi hiru no tsuki

spring peace—
Mount Asama's smoke
and the noon moon

Mount Asama is a volcano in Issa's home province of Shinano, active during the poet's lifetime. The eruption of 1783, when Issa was twenty-one years old and living in Edo, killed over a thousand people.

1820

長閑や鼠のなめる角田川
nodokasa ya nezumi no nameru sumida-gawa

spring peace—
a mouse licking up
Sumida River

year unknown

長閑さや垣間を覗く山の僧

nodokasa ya kakima wo nozoku yama no sō

spring peace—
a mountain monk peeks
through a fence

1793

嬌女を日々にかぞへる春日哉

taoyame wo hi-bi ni kazoeru haru hi kana

pretty girls multiply
day by day...
spring days!

1807

鶏の人の顔見る日永哉

niwatori no hito no kao miru hi naga kana

the chicken stares
at the man...
a long day

1808

のべの草蝶の上にも日や長き
nobe no kusa chō no ue ni mo hi ya nagaki

even for the meadow
butterflies...
the day is long

Or: "for the butterfly."

1808

ぽちやぽちやと鳩の太りて日の長き
pocha-pocha to hato no futorite hi no nagaki

roly-poly pigeons
growing fatter...
a long day

1809

永の日に口明通る烏哉
naga no hi ni kuchi ake-tōru karasu kana

in the long day
passing with mouth wide...
a crow

1812

永の日を喰やくわずや池の亀
naga no hi wo kū ya kuwazu ya ike no kame

in the long day
they eat, they don't eat
pond turtles

In a headnote for this haiku, Issa writes that he visited a secluded pond, where he watched the turtles begging for handouts. It must be painful for them, he mused, to live so long in this "world of suffering"; *IZ* 4.111.

1818

長き日や大福帳をかり枕
nagaki hi ya daifukuchō wo kari makura

a long day—
his account book serves
as a pillow

1819

白犬の眉書れたる日永哉
shiro inu no mayu kakaretaru hi naga kana

drawing eyebrows
on the white dog...
a long day

1820

大口を明て烏も日永哉

ōkuchi wo aite karasu mo hi naga kana

the crow, too
yawns and yawns...
a long day

1820

永き日や牛の涎が一里程

nagaki hi ya ushi no yodare ga ichi ri hodo

long day—
the cow's slobber
about two miles long

The cow's slobber trail stretches for about one *ri* 里 (2.44 miles).

1821

日永とて犬と烏の喧嘩哉

hi naga tote inu to karasu no kenka kana

a long day—
the dog and the crow
quarreling

1823

鶏の座敷を歩く日永哉
niwatori no zashiki wo aruku hi naga kana

a chicken strolls
through the sitting room...
a long day

1805

木兎の面魂よ春の暮
mimizuku no tsuradamashii yo haru no kure

the little owl
makes a face...
spring dusk

1804

春の夜や瓢なでても人の来る
haru no yo ya fukube nadete mo hito no kuru

spring evening—
he comes out to pet
the gourd

1806

山守や春の行方を箒して
yamamori ya haru no yukigata wo hōki shite

forest ranger—
he sweeps away spring
with a broom

1814

一村は柳の中や春の雪
hito mura wa yanagi no naka ya haru no yuki

in a village
deep in the willows...
spring snow

1822

雷の光る中より春の雪
kaminari no hikaru naka yori haru no yuki

from deep
in the lightning's flash...
spring snow falling

1803

膳先に雀なく也春の雨
zen saki ni suzume naku nari haru no ame

at my dinner tray
a sparrow chirps...
spring rain

1804

ほうろくをかぶつて行や春の雨
hōroku wo kabutte yuku ya haru no ame

walking along
a baking pan on his head...
spring rain

Or: "her head."

1804

山の鐘も一ッひびけ春の雨
yama no kane mo hitotsu hibike haru no ame

clang once more
mountain temple bell!
spring rain

1804

我松もかたじけなさや春の雨
waga matsu mo katajikenasa ya haru no ame

my pine tree too
is grateful...
spring rain

1805

春雨や家鴨よちよち門歩き
harusame ya ahiru yochi-yochi kado aruki

spring rain—
ducks waddle-waddle
to the gate

1809

神棚は皆つつじ也春の雨
kami-dana wa mina tsutsuji nari haru no ame

the little shrine
is all azaleas...
spring rain

The flowers have enveloped the little Shinto shrine. In the native Japanese religion of Shinto, nature is sacred, with in-dwelling gods. The fact that the shrine is almost invisible among the flowers suggests many things. Are the flowers themselves, in a spontaneous act of reverence, decorating the shrine, in which case their blossoms can be viewed as acts of prayer? Or, do the flowers represent the living god of the shrine, to which Issa is bowing as he writes the poem? Or...?

1809
けふもけふも同じ山見て春の雨
kyō mo kyō mo onaji yama mite haru no ame

today too
looking at the same mountain...
spring rain

1811
春雨に大欠する美人哉
harusame ni ōakubi suru bijin kana

in the spring rain
a big yawn...
pretty woman

1813

春雨や喰れ残りの鴨が鳴
harusame ya kuware-nokori no kamo ga naku

spring rain—
the uneaten ducks
are quacking

1813

春雨や鼠のなめる角田川
harusame ya nezumi no nameru sumida-gawa

spring rain—
a mouse licking up
Sumida River

1814

梟も面癖直せ春の雨
fukurō mo tsuraguse naose haru no ame

cheer up, owl!
the spring rain
is falling

In a later, undated copy from the Bunsei Era (1818-1830), Issa prefaces the poem with the headnote, "The pigeon speaks words of admonishment." Makoto Ueda believes that the owl is Issa; the pigeon is his wife, Kiku (*Dew on the Grass* 98). In his children's book, Matthew Gollub merges the headnote with the poem: "The dove tells the owl/ to fix his worried face"; *Cool Melons— Turn to Frogs! The Life and Poems of Issa* (New York: Lee and Low Books, 1998). The book's illustrator, Kazuko G. Stone, presents a charming picture of dove and owl (Kiku and Issa) as husband and wife kneeling side by side.

1816

春雨や欠をうつる門の犬
harusame ya akubi wo utsuru kado no inu

spring rain—
he catches my yawn
dog at the gate

1818

笹ツ葉の春雨なめる鼠哉
sasappa no harusame nameru nezumi kana

licking a bamboo leaf's
spring rain...
mouse

1819

朝市の大肌ぬぎや春の雨

asa ichi no ōhadanugi ya haru no ame

at morning market
he bares his chest...
spring rain

1820

春雨や妹が袂に銭の音

harusame ya imo ga tamoto ni zeni no oto

spring rain—
in my lover's sleeve
coins jingle

Imo 妹 ("sister") is a literary word for "dear one"—an intimate term that a man uses to refer to his beloved; *KDJ* 454. Might the "dear one" be Issa's wife, Kiku?

1820

春雨や猫におどりをおしえる子

harusame ya neko ni odori wo oshieru ko

spring rain—
a child gives a dance lesson
to the cat

1823

白妙の雪の上也春の雨

shirotae no yuki no ue nari haru no ame

on the white blanket
of snow...
spring rain

1810

鳩の恋烏の恋や春の雨

hato no koi karasu no koi ya haru no ame

pigeons mating
crows mating...
the spring rain falls

1825

めぐり日と俳諧日也春の雨

meguri hi to haikai hi nari haru no ame

a day for wandering
a day for haiku...
spring rain

1806

春の風垣の雑巾かわく也

haru no kaze kaki no zōkin kawaku nari

spring breeze—
the mop on the fence
drying

1807

春風に箸を掴んで寝る子哉

haru kaze ni hashi wo tsukande neru ko kana

in spring's breeze
clutching chopsticks
the sleeping child

1811

春風や牛に引かれて善光寺

haru kaze ya ushi ni hikarete zenkōji

spring breeze—
a cow leads the way
to Zenkō Temple

This haiku refers to a popular folktale in Issa's home province of Shinano. A sinful woman left a piece of cloth to dry in the garden behind her house, but a passing cow snagged it with a horn and trotted off. The woman followed the beast all the way to Zenkōji, where it disappeared and she found herself standing before the image of Amida Buddha. From that point on, she became pious.

1812

春の風足むく方へいざさらば
haru no kaze ashi muku hō e iza saraba

spring breeze—
where my feet are pointed
I'm on my way

1813

春風に尻を吹るる屋根屋哉
haru kaze ni shiri wo fukaruru yaneya kana

his butt cooled
by the spring breeze
roof thatcher

1814

春風や大宮人の野雪隠
haru kaze ya ōmiyabito no no setchin

spring breeze—
the great courtier
poops in the field

French translator Jean Cholley (correctly, I think) inter-
prets *no setchin* ("field outhouse") to mean a person doing
his business in an open field; *En village de miséreux* 167.

1820

狗が鼠とる也はるの風
enokoro ga nezumi toru nari haru no kaze

the puppy has caught
a mouse...
spring breeze

1822

春風に肩衣かけて御供かな
harukaze ni kataginu kakete o-tomo kana

in spring breeze
his stole billowing...
a monk comes too

The "billowing" in my translation makes explicit what Issa's Japanese might only imply. Issa states simply that the stole is "hanging" (*kakete* かけて) on the monk's body. Putting this fact with the spring breeze, I picture it billowing.

1822

春風に猿もおや子の湯治哉

haru kaze ni saru mo oyako no tōji kana

spring breeze—
monkey families, too
take healing baths

Issa is referring to an outdoor hot spring.

1822

春風に吹出されたる道者かな

harukaze ni fuki-dasaretaru dōja kana

blown forth
by the spring breeze...
pilgrims

Or: "the pilgrim."

1824

春風や三人乗りのもどり馬
haru kaze ya sannin nori no modori uma

spring breeze—
three ride the same horse
home

1826

春風や野道につづく浅黄傘
haru kaze ya nomichi ni tsuzuku asagi-gasa

spring breeze—
across the field a parade
of pale blue parasols

year unknown

春風や歩行ながらの御法談
haru kaze ya aruki nagara no ōhōdan

spring breeze—
the priest gives his sermon
walking along

1805

春の月軒の雫の又おちよ

haru no tsuki noki no shizuku no mata ochi yo

the spring moon
in a raindrop from the eaves...
falls again

1795

朧々ふめば水也まよひ道

oboro-oboro fumeba mizu nari mayoi michi

in hazy night
stepping into water...
losing my way

The season word in this haiku, *oboro* 朧, refers succinctly to a hazy night of spring. In this uncertain, dreamlike light, Issa steps off a path into water. In *Saigoku kikō* ("Western Provinces Travel Diary") Issa provides an explanatory note for which Shinji Ogawa offers this paraphrase: after hearing of his priest friend Sarai's death, Issa begged his replacement for a night's stay at the temple but was refused; *IZ* 5.36.

1790

三文が霞見にけり遠眼鏡
san mon ga kasumi mi ni keri tōmegane

for three pennies
nothing but mist...
telescope

1794

きぬぎぬやかすむ迄見る妹が家
kinu-ginu ya kasumu made miru imo ga ie

lovers parting—
looking back at her house
until only mist

This unusually romantic haiku has the headnote, "Parting lovers." On the morning after a night of passion, lovers depart.

1795

朝がすみ天守の雨戸聞へけり
asa-gasumi tenshu no amado kikoe keri

morning mist—
the castle's shutters
bang open

1804

霞み行や二親持し小すげ笠
kasumi yuku ya futa oya mochishi ko suge-gasa

walking in mist
in a little sedge hat
with both parents

1805

鰯焼片山畠や薄がすみ
iwashi yaku kata yama hata ya usu-gasumi

grilling sardines
in a mountain field...
thin mist

1808

玉琴も乞食の笛もかすみけり
tamagoto mo kojiki no fue mo kasumi keri

a precious harp
a beggar's flute
deep in mist

1811

彼の桃が流れ来よ来よ春がすみ
ka no momo ga nagare ki yo ki yo harugasumi

O peach
come float to me!
spring mist

According to R. H. Blyth in *Haiku*, a woman was washing clothes by a stream, "when a huge peach (*momo* 桃) came floating down. She took it home, and when she and her husband cut it open, they found a little boy, Momotarō, inside" (Tokyo: Hokuseido, 1949-1952; rpt. 1981-1982/reset paperback edition) 2.418. The fairy tale of the floating Peach Boy makes the haiku moment even more magical. The spring mist is so thick, Issa fancies that the peach, like the baby boy of the story, might come floating to his hand.

1812

かすむ日の咄するやらのべの馬
kasumu hi no hanashi suru yara nobe no uma

on a misty day
they chat...
horses in the field

1812

かすむ日やさぞ天人の御退屈
kasumu hi ya sazo tennin no o-taikutsu

misty day—
no doubt Heaven's saints
bored stiff

This haiku is poem six of Issa's six-poem series on the Six Ways of Buddhist reincarnation.

year unknown

ほくほくと霞んで来るはどなた哉
hoku-hoku to kasunde kuru wa donata kana

rap-a-tap
who's that coming
in the mist?

I imagine a cane clacking.

1814

野ばくちや藪の法談も一かすみ
no bakuchi ya yabu no dangi mo hito kasumi

gambling in the field
a sermon in the thicket...
one mist

year unknown

けふもけふもかすんで暮らす小家哉

kyō mo kyō mo kasunde kurasu ko ie kana

today too, today too
living in mist...
little house

1817

笠でするさらばさらばや薄がすみ

kasa de suru saraba saraba ya usu-gasumi

waving umbrella-hats
farewell! farewell!
thin mist

This is the first haiku that Issa wrote in Second Month, 1817. It has the headnote, "Spring Colors at Karuizawa." In his book *Issa to onnatachi* 一茶と女達 ("Issa and Women"), Kobayashi Masafumi believes that the scene describes two lovers parting in the morning, more particularly, a man (possibly Issa) and his *ichiyazuma* 一夜妻 ("one night wife"): a prostitute or temporary consort (Tokyo: Sanwa 2004) 44.

1819

かすむ日やしんかんとして大座敷
kasumu hi ya shinkan to shite ōzashiki

misty day—
a hush in the big
sitting room

1820

後供はかすみ引けり加賀の守
atodomo wa kasumi hiki keri kaga no kami

his attendants behind
haul the mist...
Lord Kaga

This haiku refers to the daimyō Maeda, Lord of Kaga. There is such a long, long line of servants hauling his possessions, it seems as if they are carrying even the far mist. Shinji Ogawa detects social criticism in this haiku: the feudal lord owns so much while common people are starving to death. The criticism, he notes, is subtle "because it was so danger- ous...subject to capital punishment."

1821

御仏と一所に霞む天窓かな
mi-hotoke to isshō ni kasumu atama kana

me and Buddha—
our heads
in the mist

1822

傘の雫もかすむ都哉
karakasa no shizuku mo kasumu miyako kana

paper umbrellas
dripping...
misty Kyoto

1822

盗人のかすんでげけら笑ひかな
nusubito no kasunde gekera warai kana

in thick spring mist
the burglar
laughing

1822

法談の手つきもかすむ御堂かな
hōdan no tetsuki mo kasumu midō kana

the preacher's
hand gestures too...
lost in temple mist

1812

陽炎に何やら猫の寝言哉
kagerō ni nani yara neko no negoto kana

heat shimmers—
how the cat talks
in her sleep!

Or: "in his sleep." "Heat shimmers" (*kagerō* 陽炎) are the wavy bends in the air that one sometimes sees in the distance on a warm day—a phenomenon associated with springtime in Japan.

1813

陽炎や子に迷ふ鶏の遠歩き
kagerō ya ko ni mayou tori no tō aruki

heat shimmers—
the child's lost chicken
struts in the distance

1816

陽炎にまぎれ込だる伏家哉

kagerō ni magire kondaru fuseya kana

vanishing
in the heat shimmers...
my humble hut

1820

さほ姫の染損なひや斑山

saohime no some sokonai madara yama

the goddess of spring
missed a few spots...
mottled mountain

Saohime and her sister, Tatsutahime, were Chinese imports, not part of the native Japanese pantheon. Saohime ruled spring; Tatsutahime, autumn. Saohime's particular task was to supervise the greening of fields and mountains. However, in the case of this particular mountain, her dyeing job has been spotty.

1810

片隅に烏かたまる雪げかな
kata sumi ni karasu katamaru yukige kana

in one spot
the crows congregate...
snow is melting!

1814

雪とけて村一ぱいの子ども哉
yuki tokete mura ippai no kodomo kana

snow melting
the village brimming over...
with children!

A master joke-teller, Issa sets up the situation in this famous haiku: "snow melting/ the village brimming over..." and then hits the reader with the unexpected punch line: "with children!" The children have been cooped inside during the long, cold winter. Now, as the snow melts, they burst outside, "flooding" the village, shouting and laughing.

1815

我庵や貧乏がくしの雪とける
waga io ya bimbō gakushi no yuki tokeru

my hut—
the poverty-hiding snow
melts away

1818

雪解や貧乏町の痩せ子達
yuki-doke ya bimbō machi no yase kodachi

snow melting—
the thin children
of the slum

1819

愛らしく両手の跡の残る雪
airashiku ryōte no ato no nokoru yuki

lovely—
in the leftover snow
both handprints

1822

小便の穴だらけ也残り雪

shōben no ana darake nari nokori yuki

riddled with piddle
the last
snow pile

1822

のら猫の爪とぐ程や残る雪

nora neko no tsume togu hodo ya nokoru yuki

the stray cat
sharpens his nails...
last snow pile

1822

みだ堂にすがりて雪の残りけり

mida dō ni sugarite yuki no nokori keri

on Amida Buddha's
temple clinging...
leftover snow

According to Pure Land Buddhism, the only possible way to achieve enlightenment involves clinging to Amida Buddha. With this in mind, the haiku reveals itself to be a parable: we are like snow melting quickly and inevitably to oblivion. All we can do is let go of the fiction of ego-control, cling to Buddha, and trust.

year unknown
親犬が瀬踏してけり雪げ川
oya inu ga sebumi shite keri yukigegawa

mother dog
testing the depth...
snow-melt river

1812
小酒屋の出現したり春の山
ko sakaya no shutsugen shitari haru no yama

the little tavern
open for business...
spring mountain

1820
相伴に我らもごろり涅槃哉
shōban ni warera mo gorori nehan kana

joining in
we curl to sleep too...
reclining Buddha

This comic haiku refers to the Second Month, fifteenth day festival of Buddha's Death Day, commemorating Gautama Buddha's entrance into nirvana (i.e., his death). Following the example set by the statue of a reclining Buddha, Issa and his companions sleep also.

1818

雨に雪しどろもどろのひがん哉
ame ni yuki shidoro-modoro no higan kana

a confusing mix
of rain and snow...
spring equinox

1820

彼岸とて袖に這する虱かな
higan tote sode ni hawasuru shirami kana

in honor of the equinox
crawling into my sleeve...
a louse

1823

五十里の江戸を出代る子ども哉

go jū ri no edo wo degawaru kodomo kana

a hundred miles to Edo
and his new job...
the child servant

In springtime, old servants were replaced by young ones. The old ones would leave their employers to return to their home villages; the young ones traveled in the opposite direction. Literally, the child must travel 50 *ri*: 122 miles (196.5 kilometers). When he was a child of fifteen, Issa left his home province on a longer journey of 240 kilometers to Edo.

1807

角力取も雛祭に遊びけり

sumotori mo hina matsuri ni asobi keri

even the sumo wrestler
has a blast...
Doll Festival

This haiku refers to the Doll Festival, the third day of Third Month, also known as "Girls' Festival."

1808

煙たいとおぼしめすかよ雛顔

kebutai to oboshimesu ka yo hiina kao

do you think
it's too smoky in here?
face of the doll

1818

いとこ雛孫雛と名の付合ふ

itoko hina mago hina to na no tsuki tamau

"Cousin Doll"
and "Grandchild Doll"
she names them

1819

片すみに煤け雛も夫婦哉

kata sumi ni susuke hiina mo meoto kana

in one corner
soot-covered dolls...
husband and wife

1822

雛達に咄しかける子ども哉
hina-dachi ni hanashi shikakeru kodomo kana

giving her dolls
a good talking-to...
the child

1824

古雛やがらくた店の日向ぼこ
furu hina ya garakuta tana no hinata-boko

the old doll
in the junk store window
sunning herself

1815

草餅や臼の中から蛙鳴
kusamochi ya usu no naka kara kawazu naku

herb cakes—
inside the mixing tub
a croaking frog

1812

米蒔くも罪ぞよ鶏がけあふぞよ

kome maku mo tsumi zo yo tori ga keau zo yo

even tossing rice
is a sin...
sparring chickens

Feeding the birds is a "sin" (*tsumi* 罪), for it has caused a violent kicking match (*keau* けあふ) among them. This haiku appears with a long headnote: "On a temple-visit to Tōkaiji in Fuse [no Benten], chickens followed me inexpediently. At a house in front of the temple gate, I bought just a bit of rice, which I scattered among the violets and dandelions. Before long though, a fight broke out. Meanwhile, groups of pigeons and sparrows came flying down from the branches, eating with tranquil hearts, but when the chickens returned, back to the trees they quickly fled. The pigeons and sparrows would have liked the kicking-fight to have lasted longer. Samurai, farmers, artizans, and merchants all make their living in this manner" (*IZ* 6.52). Issa views the squabbling birds at the temple gate as a microcosm of human society.

1804

女から先へかすむぞ汐干がた
onna kara saki e kasumu zo shiohigata

the mist covers up
the women first...
shell gathering

1804

汐干潟雨しとしとと暮かかる
shiohi-gata ame shito-shito to kure kakaru

low tide
in a soft, soft rain...
darkness coming

The season word ("tideland at low tide": *shiohi-gata* 汐干潟) suggests that there are people in the scene, hunched over, searching for shellfish. The day is growing dark, and rain is falling. Issa evokes a slice of life, with a world of feeling and implications, with a few deft strokes of his writing brush.

1816

のさのさと汐干案内や里の犬
nosa-nosa to shiohi anai ya sato no inu

my intrepid guide
on the low tide beach...
village dog

1824

ふらんどや桜の花をもちながら
furando ya sakura no hana wo mochi nagara

swinging on the swing
clutching
cherry blossoms

1813

草つみや羽織の上になく蛙
kusa tsumi ya haori no ue ni naku kawazu

picking herbs—
on my coat a croaking
frog

1816

正面はおばば組也茶つみ唄

shōmen wa o-baba-gumi nari cha tsumi uta

led by a gang
of grannies...
the tea-picking song

1818

僧正が音頭とる也茶つみ唄

sōjō ga ondo toru nari cha tsumi uta

the high priest
joins right in...
tea-picking song

1805

うつくしい鳥見し当よ山をやく

utsukushii tori mishi ate yo yama wo yaku

where I saw
a pretty bird...
they burn the mountain

Fires were set in the mountains to clear away dead brush and
prepare the fields for tilling.

99

1793

命也焼く野の虫を拾ふ鳥
inochi nari yaku no no mushi wo hirou tori

such is life—
the burning field's bugs
a feast for birds

1814

烏等も恋をせよとてやく野哉
karasura mo koi wo seyo tote yaku no kana

make love, crows
while you can!
burning fields

1819

ざくざくと雪かき交ぜて田打哉
zaku-zaku to yuki kakimazete ta uchi kana

crunch! crunch!
plowing the rice field
snow

1814

畠打の真似して歩く烏哉
hata uchi no mane shite aruku karasu kana

mocking the farmer
plowing, the strutting
crow

The crow seems to be humorously imitating the farmer,
walking behind him.

1823

畠打や通してくれる寺参
hata uchi ya tōshite kureru tera mairi

the plowman lets me
cross his field...
temple pilgrimage

1824

菊畠や一打ごとに酒五盃
kiku hata ya hito uchi goto ni sake go hai

chrysanthemum garden—
one chop of the hoe
five cups of sake

Though Issa doesn't specify the farm implement, it is

apparently a sort of hoe.

1812

山鳥おれがつぎ木を笑ふ哉
yama-garasu ore ga tsugiki wo warau kana

the mountain crow
laughs at the branch
I grafted

1805

山猫や恋から直に里馴るる
yama neko ya koi kara sugu ni sato naruru

wild cat—
after making love
he's the town pet

1809

恋猫の源氏めかする垣根哉
koi neko no genji mekasuru kakine kana

the lover cat
dandied up like Genji
at the fence

The haiku spoofs a scene from *The Tale of Genji* by Murasaki

Shikibu (Chapter 5), wherein Prince Genji peers through a wattle fence and catches sight of ten-year old Murasaki. Later that year he abducts her and begins training her to be his ideal woman. Issa's sly poem can be seen to elevate the mate-seeking cat—by equating him with an archetypal romantic lover—and yet also to denigrate Genji, suggesting slyly that the "shining prince" was just a sexually excited animal, in fact, a predator.

1812

猫なくや中を流るる角田川
neko naku ya naka wo nagaruru sumida-gawa

cats' love calls—
between them flows
Sumida River

Two cats ready for lovemaking are separated by the wide river. This haiku alludes to the Tanabata legend, according to which two lovers (the stars Altair and Vega) are tragically separated by "Heaven's River," the Milky Way.

1812

火の上を上手にとぶはうかれ猫
hi no ue wo jyōzu ni tobu wa ukare neko

jumping so well
over the fire...
the love-crazed cat

103

1815

鼻先に飯粒つけて猫の恋

hana saki ni meshi tsubu tsukete neko no koi

a grain of rice
stuck to his nose...
lover cat

1817

有明にかこち顔也夫婦猫

ariake ni kakochi kao nari meoto neko

at daybreak
what grouchy faces...
Mr. and Mrs. Cat

Is the honeymoon over?

1817

うかれきて鶏追まくる男猫哉

ukare kite tori oimakuru oneko kana

so love-crazed
he chases a chicken...
tomcat

1818

ばか猫や縛れながら恋を鳴く

baka neko ya shibarare nagara koi wo naku

fool cat
though tethered still crying
for love

1822

大猫が恋草臥の鼾かな

ōneko ga koi kutabire no ibiki kana

the big cat
worn out from lovemaking
snores

1817

親としてかくれんぼする子猫哉

oya to shite kakurenbo suru ko neko kana

mother cat
plays hide-and-seek...
with her kittens

1818

猫の子や秤にかかりつつざれる

neko no ko ya hakari ni kakari tsutsu zareru

the kitten
being weighed in the scales
keeps playing

1823

女猫子ゆゑの盗とく逃よ

onna neko ko yue no nusumi toku nige yo

mother cat
steals for her kittens...
run faster!

1824

猫の子の十が十色の毛なみ哉

neko no ko no tō ga to iro no kenami kana

ten kittens
ten
different colors

1824

さをしかや社壇に角を奉る
saoshika ya shadan ni tsuno wo tatematsuru

on the shrine's altar
the buck offers
his antlers

Issa's image of a buck shedding his antlers on a temple mountain is symbolic. Like monks who shave their heads, the buck seems to be relinquishing worldliness. Shedding the weapons with which he earlier battered rivals in the struggle to win and keep a mate further suggests the notion of celibacy. The buck, Issa hints, has become a monk, taking his first step on the road to enlightenment.

year unknown

雀子や人が立ても口を明く
suzumego ya hito ga tatte mo kuchi wo aku

baby sparrow—
even when people come
opening his mouth

1804

雀子も梅に口明く念仏哉

suzumego mo ume ni kuchi aku nebutsu kana

sparrow babies
in plum blossoms
praise Buddha!

1812

親雀子雀山もいさむぞよ

oya suzume ko suzume yama mo isamu zo yo

parent sparrows
baby sparrows...
a happy mountain

1813

大仏の鼻で鳴也雀の子

daibutsu no hana de naku nari suzume no ko

in the great bronze
Buddha's nose chirping...
sparrow babies

1819

我と来て遊べや親のない雀
ware to kite asobe ya oya no nai suzume

come and play
with me...
orphan sparrow

This is a reference to Issa's own stepchild past. In its original form (1814) the sparrow is "coming to play" (*kite asobu* 来て 遊ぶ). In this rewrite, Issa changes the verb to a command: "come and play" (*kite asobe* 来て遊べ). This second version is more popular in Japan—memorized by schoolchildren nationwide.

1816

子どもらの披露に歩く雀哉
kodomora no hirō ni aruku suzume kana

introducing their children
to society...
strutting sparrows

1819

大勢の子を連歩く雀哉

ōzei no ko wo tsure aruku suzume kana

a troop of children
march behind her...
mother sparrow

1819

雀の子そこのけそこのけ御馬が通る

suzume no ko soko noke soko noke o-uma ga tōru

baby sparrows
move aside!
Sir Horse passes

In Issa's Japan peasants had to grovel by the roadside when feudal lords (*daimyō* 大名) passed.

1823

牢屋から出たり入つたり雀の子

rōya kara detari ittari suzume no ko

in and out
of prison it goes...
baby sparrow

Or: "they go...baby sparrows."

1824

慈悲すれば糞をする也雀の子

jihi sureba hako wo suru nari suzume no ko

when you hold him kindly
he poops on you...
baby sparrow

1825

雀子や牛にも馬にも踏れずに

suzumego ya ushi ni mo uma ni mo fumarezu ni

baby sparrows
by the cow and the horse
untrampled

1808

鶯にだまつて居らぬ雀かな

uguisu ni damatte oranu suzume kana

not hushing up
for the nightingale...
sparrows

Or: "sparrow." The fact that the plebian sparrow(s) will not hush for the princely nightingale makes for a moment of humor as well as social satire. Issa's sympathies, of course, lie with the sparrows.

1811

鶯の足をふく也梅の花

uguisu no ashi wo fuku nari ume no hana

the nightingale
wipes his feet...
on plum blossoms

1813

鶯にあてがつておく垣ね哉

uguisu ni ategatte oku kakine kana

nightingale
this fence is reserved
for you

1814

赤い実を咥た所が鶯ぞ

akai mi wo kuwaeta toko ga uguisu zo

a red berry
in its beak posing...
nightingale

1814

鶯が呑ぞ浴るぞ割下水
uguisu ga nomu zo abiru zo wari gesui

the nightingale
drinks and bathes...
sewage canal

1814

なけよなけ下手鶯もおれが窓
nake yo nake heta uguisu mo ore ga mado

sing! sing!
off-key nightingale
at my window

1815

鶯や雨だらけなる朝の声
uguisu ya ame darake naru asa no koe

nightingale—
his rain-drenched
morning voice

1815

鶯よ何百鳴いた飯前に
uguisu yo nan-byaku naita meshimae ni

nightingale—
how many hundreds of songs
before you eat?

1818

鶯や垣踏んで見ても一声
uguisu ya kaki funde mite mo hitotsu koe

nightingale—
even strutting on the fence
a song

1818

薮超の乞食笛よ鶯よ
yabu goshi no kojiki fue yo uguisu yo

wafting through trees
a beggar's flute
a nightingale's song

1820

鶯や弥陀の浄土の東門

uguisu ya mida no jōdo no higashi kado

a nightingale sings—
the east gate
of Amida's Pure Land

Since the mythical Pure Land is located in the far west, its east gate would be the nearest one to this world, i.e. its entrance. The nightingale seems to coax the listener to Paradise here-and-now. This haiku has the headnote, "Tennōji" (Tennō Temple).

1821

鶯やあきらめのよい籠の声

uguisu ya akirame no yoi kago no koe

the nightingale
resigned to his fate...
voice in a cage

1824

鶯や御前へ出ても同じ声
uguisu ya gozen e dete mo onaji koe

nightingale—
for the emperor too
the same song

1815

急度した宿もなくて夕乙鳥
kitto shita yado mo nakute yū tsubame

no definite place
to spend the night...
evening swallow

Or: "evening swallows." French translator Jean Cholley chooses the plural; *En village de miséreux* 135. I prefer to picture a single swallow making its way across the evening sky: a lone traveler, like Issa.

1822

大仏の鼻から出たる乙鳥哉
daibutsu no hana kara detaru tsubame kana

from the great bronze
Buddha's nose...
a swallow!

1824

鶏の隣をかりるつばめ哉

niwatori no tonari wo kariru tsubame kana

renting a place
next door to the chickens...
swallows

1826

乙鳥子·のけいこにとぶや馬の尻

tsubame-go no keiko ni tobu ya uma no shiri

the baby swallow's
flying lesson...
off the horse's rump

Or: "to the horse's rump."

1795

天に雲雀人間海にあそぶ日ぞ

ten ni hibari ningen umi ni asobu hi zo

larks in the sky
people in the sea...
a holiday

1812

細ろ次のおくは海也なく雲雀
hosoroji no oku wa umi nari naku hibari

down a narrow alley
the ocean...
a singing lark

1813

昼飯をたべに下りたる雲雀哉
hirumeshi wo tabe ni oritaru hibari kana

coming down
to eat his lunch...
skylark

1818

小島にも畠打也鳴雲雀
kojima ni mo hatake utsunari naku hibari

on a tiny island, too
plowing
to the lark's song

1822

おりおりに子を見廻つては雲雀哉

ori-ori ni ko wo mi-mawatte wa hibari kana

circling now and then
to eye the children...
skylark

1824

鶏にさらばさらばと雲雀哉

niwatori ni saraba saraba to hibari kana

farewell! farewell!
to the chicken...
the skylark flies away

1808

尻尾から月の出かかる雉哉

shippo kara tsuki no dekakaru kigisu kana

its tail points
to the rising moon...
pheasant

1812

雉うろうろうろ門を覗くぞよ

kigisu uro-uro-uro kado wo nozoku zoyo

a pheasant
loitering about, peeks
in my gate

1814

一星見つけたやうにきじの鳴

hitotsu boshi mitsuketa yō ni kiji no naku

as if it just spotted
a star
the pheasant cries

1820

さをしかのせなかをかりて雉の鳴

saoshika no senaka wo karite kiji no naku

borrowing the buck's
back, the pheasant
cries

1823

引明や鶏なき里の雉の声
hikiake ya tori naki sato no kiji no koe

daybreak—
in a rooster-less village
a pheasant's cry

1803

行灯で飯くふ人やかへる雁
andon de meshi kuu hito ya kaeru kari

eating my rice
by lamplight...
the geese depart

1806

行雁や更科見度望みさへ
yuku kari ya sarashina mitai nozomi sae

geese fly north—
how they yearn to see
Mount Sarashina

Mount Sarashina is another name for Ubasute or Obasute, a mountain in Issa's home province of Shinano where old people were, according to legend, "thrown away": left to die.

Today it is called Kamurikiyama.

1804

かへる雁翌はいづくの月や見る

kaeru kari asu wa izuku no tsuki ya miru

departing geese
where will you moon-gaze
tomorrow?

Issa implies that the wild geese are just like haiku poets: they, just like he, travel restlessly, forever seeking ideal places in which to gaze at the moon.

1804

一ッでも鳴て行也かへる雁

hitotsu demo naite yuku nari kaeru kari

just one
but he goes honking...
departing goose

1807

立雁が大きな糞をしたりけり

tatsu kari ga ōkina hako wo shitari keri

the departing goose
drops an enormous
crap

1807

行雁や人の心もうはの空

yuku kari ya hito no kokoro mo uwa no sora

traveling geese—
the human heart, too
wanders

1813

行な雁どつこも茨のうき世ぞや

yuku na kari dokko mo bara no ukiyo zo ya

don't go geese!
everywhere it's a floating world
of sorrow

1820

すつぽんも羽ほしげ也帰る雁
suppon mo hane hoshige nari kaeru kari

even the turtle
wants feathers...
the geese depart

1822

大組の後やだまつて帰る雁
ōgumi no ato ya damatte kaeru kari

after the big flock
silence...
geese flying north

1791

青梅に手をかけて寝る蛙哉
aoume ni te wo kakete neru kawazu kana

resting his hands
on the green plum, asleep...
a frog

1803

かりそめの娉入月よやなく蛙
karisome no yomeri tsuki yo ya naku kawazu

a fleeting moonlit
wedding night...
frogs singing

This haiku has the headnote, *cho* 著 (in Chinese, pronounced *zhu*) a word that means a "literary work." It is the title of Song 98 from the most ancient collection of Chinese poetry, *Shi Jing* of the Zhou Dynasty. It is written from the point of view of a young woman, and begins with the line, "He was waiting for me between the door and the screen." In Eighth and Ninth Month of 1803 Issa wrote a series of over thirty haiku inspired by poems from *Shi Jing* (*IZ* 2.117-31). This one alludes to a brief but romantic night of love but comically replaces the human lovers with frogs.

1803

つるべにも一夜過ぎけりなく蛙
tsurube ni mo hito yo sugi keri naku kawazu

even in the well bucket
croaking all night...
a frog

This haiku has the headnote, "Heaven, Wind, Coupling": a

reference to Chinese divination, specifically to Hexagram 44 of the *I Ching*. When Heaven (*Qian* 天) is the upper trigram and Wind (*Xun* 風) is the lower, the resulting hexagram is *Gou* 姤, the sign for copulation or "coming to meet." Issa's geomantic joke is on the frog, singing his mating song all night, eager to copulate, yet without much chance of success inside the well bucket.

1805

入相は蛙の目にも涙哉
iriai wa kawazu no me ni mo namida kana

sunset—
tears shine in a frog's eyes
too

1807

影ぼふし我にとなりし蛙哉
kagebōshi ware ni tonari shi kawazu kana

next to my shadow
that
of a frog

1812

小便の滝を見せうぞ鳴蛙

shōben no taki wo mishō zo naku kawazu

get ready to see
my piss waterfall!
croaking frog

1812

どち向も万吉とやなく蛙

dochi muku mo yorozu yoshi to ya naku kawazu

in every direction
ten thousand blessings...
croaking frogs

1812

橋わたる盲の跡の蛙哉

hashi wataru mekura no ato no kawazu kana

crossing the bridge
behind the blind man...
a frog

The figure of a blind man crossing a bridge recalls a series of at least eight *zenga* (Zen paintings) by Hakuin Ekaku (1685-1768). In these monochrome paintings, the number of blind men on the bridge ranges from one to nine; see Audrey Yoshiko Seo and Stephan Addiss, *The Sound of One Hand: Paintings and Calligraphy by Zen Master Hakuin* (Boston: Shambhala 2010) 139-41. The blind men, moving from right to left, strive to leave the world behind and reach, on the other side of the precarious bridge, enlightenment. In Issa's haiku, the blind man's faithful follower toward enlightenment is a frog.

1813

ちる花にあごを並べる蛙哉
chiru hana ni ago wo naraberu kawazu kana

chin-deep
in the fallen blossoms...
a frog

1813

むきむきに蛙のいとこはとこ哉
muki muki ni kawazu no itoko hatoko kana

facing every-which way
frog cousins
and second cousins!

1813

いうぜんとして山を見る蛙哉
iuzen to shite yama wo miru kawazu kana

serene and still
the mountain-viewing
frog

This haiku appears in *Hachiban nikki* 八番日記 ("Eighth Diary") without headnote, but Issa recopies it six years later in *Oraga haru* with a prose preface: "In the summer evening, spreading my straw mat, I call 'Lucky! Lucky!' and soon he comes crawling out from his hiding place in the thicket, enjoying the evening cool just like a person." Issa's first two phrases echo a well-known, pre-Tang Chinese poem by Tao Qian, also known as Tao Yuanming. His poem, "I Built My House Near Where Others Dwell," has the lines, "I pluck chrysanthemums under the eastern hedge,/ And gaze afar towards the southern mountains." The ancient Chinese poem is about a hermit poet gazing upon distant mountains and flying birds, sensing within these things an ineffable "hint of Truth"; see William Acker, *T'ao the Hermit, Sixty Poems by T'ao Chi'en* (London: Thames and Hudson, 1952) 66.

1815

亀どのに負さつて鳴蛙哉
kame dono ni obusatte naku kawazu kana

hitching a ride
on Mr. Turtle...
a croaking frog

1815

天下泰平と居並ぶ蛙かな
tenka taihei to i-narabu kawazu kana

sitting in a row
peace on earth...
frogs

1816

小仏の御首からも蛙かな
ko-botoke no o-kashira kara mo kawazu kana

the little Buddha's head
a launch pad too...
frogs

1816

痩蛙まけるな一茶是に有り
yasegaeru makeru na issa kore ni ari

scrawny frog, hang tough!
Issa
is here

One of Issa's most famous and beloved haiku, he wrote it at Ganshoin temple in Obuse, Nagano Prefecture. In his diary, he explains, "I stooped to watch a frog scuffle on the 20th day of Fourth Month." Since he likes to describe himself as impoverished and hungry, Issa feels a special kinship with the scrawny frog.

1816

我庵に用ありそうな蛙哉
waga io ni yō ari sōna kawazu kana

in my hut
on urgent business...
a frog

1819

おれとして白眼くらする蛙かな
ore to shite niramikura suru kawazu kana

locked in a staring contest
me...
and a frog

Issa produced two manuscripts of *Hachiban nikki*, and this haiku appears in both, though in slightly different versions. In both versions the haiku is prefaced with the phrase, "Sitting alone."

1819

親分と見えて上座に鳴蛙
oyabun to miete jōza ni naku kawazu

looks like the boss
in the seat of honor...
croaking frog

1824

掌に蛙を居るらかん哉
tenohira ni kawazu wo sueru rakan kana

a frog squats
in his open palm...
a holy man

1824

天文を考へ顔の蛙哉

temmon wo kangae kao no kawazu kana

with a face
like he's contemplating the stars...
a frog

1825

じつとして馬に嗅るる蛙哉

jitto shite uma ni kagaruru kawazu kana

stone still
for the smelling horse...
a frog

1788

舞蝶にしばしは旅も忘けり

mau chō ni shibashi wa tabi mo wasure keri

dancing butterflies—
my journey forgotten
for a while

1804

初蝶のいきおひ猛に見ゆる哉

hatsu chō no ikioi mou ni miyuru kana

the year's first
butterfly
full of swagger

1805

我庵は蝶の寝所とゆふべ哉

waga io wa chō no nedoko to yūbe kana

my hut
the butterfly's sleeping place
tonight

うつつなの人の迷ひや野べの蝶

utsutsuna no hito no mayoi ya nobe no chō

casting a spell
on the man...
meadow butterflies

1806

門々を一々巡る小てふ哉

kado kado wo ichi-ichi meguru ko chō kana

gate after gate
making the rounds...
little butterfly

1806

蝶ひらひら仏のひざをもどる也

chō hira-hira hotoke no hiza wo modoru nari

flitting butterfly
to Buddha's lap
returns

1811

むつまじや生れかはらばのべの蝶

mutsumaji ya umare kawaraba nobe no chō

such sweet harmony
to be reborn
a meadow butterfly!

1812

猪ねらふ腕にすがる小てふ哉
shishi nerau kaina ni sugaru ko chō kana

clinging to
the boar hunter's arm...
little butterfly

1812

蝶まふや鹿の最期の矢の先に
chō mau ya shika no saigo no ya no saki ni

butterfly dances
'round the arrow
in a dying deer

1812

鉄砲の三尺先の小てふかな
teppō no san jaku saki no ko chō kana

three feet
from the musket's barrel...
little butterfly

1812

寺山や児はころげる蝶はとぶ

tera yama ya chigo wa korogeru chō wa tobu

temple mountain—
a baby tumbles
a butterfly flits

1812

夜明から小てふの夫婦かせぎ哉

yoake kara ko chō no meoto kasegi kana

from dawn to dusk
the butterfly couple
makes their living

1813

てふ小てふ小蝶の中の山家哉

chō ko chō ko chō no naka no yamaga kana

amid butterflies
little butterflies
mountain home

1813

丸く寝た犬にべつたり小てふ哉
maruku neta inu ni bettari ko chō kana

stuck to the dog
curled asleep...
little butterfly

1814

蝶べたりあみだ如来の頬べたへ
chō betari amida nyorai no hobbeta e

a butterfly
stuck fast to Amida
Buddha's cheek

1814

べつたりと蝶の咲たる枯木哉
bettari to chō no sakitaru kareki kana

blooming
with butterflies
the dead tree

The tree isn't technically dead but leafless and dry (*kareki* 枯木).

1815

此方が善光寺とや蝶のとぶ

kono kata ga zenkōji to ya chō no tobu

"Follow me to Zenkō Temple!"
a butterfly
flits

1815

鹿の角かりて休みし小てふ哉

shika no tsuno karite yasumishi ko chō kana

borrowing an antler
the little butterfly
rests

1816

馬の耳一日なぶる小てふ哉

uma no mimi ichi nichi naburu ko chō kana

all day teasing
the horse's ear...
little butterfly

1816

湯入衆の頭かぞへる小てふ哉

yu iri shū no atama kazoeru ko chō kana

counting heads
in a hot tub...
little butterfly

1818

祝ひ日や白い僧達白い蝶

iwai-bi ya shiroi sōtachi shiroi chō

festival day—
white robed monks
and a white butterfly

Or: "white butterflies."

1819

てふてふのふはりととんだ茶釜哉

chōchō no fuwari to tonda chagama kana

the butterfly's
soft landing...
in the tea kettle!

Issa copies this haiku in one of his journals with the headnote, "Morin Temple"—a Buddhist temple that houses a legendary tea kettle; *IZ* 6.170, note 142. This so-called "Good Luck Tea Kettle" was actually a badger in disguise.

1820

枕する腕に蝶の寝たりけり
makura suru kahina ni chō no netari keri

my arm
for its pillow
the butterfly sleeps

1821

野ばくちの銭の中より小蝶哉
no bakuchi no zeni no naka yori ko chō kana

gambling in the field—
from the pot
a little butterfly

1825

過去のやくそくかよ袖に寝小てふ
kako no yakusoku ka yo sode ni neru ko chō

a previous life's bond?
little butterfly
on my sleeve, asleep

year unknown
庭のてふ子が這へばとびはへばとぶ
niwa no chō ko ga haeba tobi haeba tobu

garden butterfly—
the child crawls, it flies
crawls, it flies...

1821
蜂の巣の隣をかりる雀哉
hachi no su no tonari wo kariru susume kana

renting a spot
next to the beehive...
sparrows

夕月や鍋の中にて鳴田にし
yūzuki ya nabe no naka nite naku tanishi

evening moon—
pond snails singing
in the kettle

This haiku has the headnote, "Hell." It is the first poem of one version of Issa's six-poem series on the Six Ways of Buddhist reincarnation. The present haiku appears only in the posthumously published 1829 version. Shinji Ogawa believes that the "singing" is the sound of the snails spitting water.

1810
蛤の芥を吐する月夜かな
hamaguri no gomi wo hakasuru tsuki yo kana

letting clams
vomit mud...
a moonlit night

year unknown
蛤や在鎌倉の雁鴎
hamaguri ya zai-kamakura no kari kamome

O clams
meet the geese and gulls
of Greater Kamakura!

year unknown
若草や今の小町が尻の跡
wakakusa ya ima no komachi ga shiri no ato

baby grass—
the stylish woman leaves
her butt print

1788

淋しさはどちら向ても菫かな
sabishisa wa dochira muite mo sumire kana

solitude—
whichever way I turn...
violets!

1815

菜の花やふはと鼠のとまりけり
na no hana ya fuwa to nezumi no tomari keri

on flowering mustard
sitting so lightly...
a mouse

Mustard (*na no hana* 菜の花, also called rape and canola) is a bright yellow flowering oil seed plant.

year unknown
菜の花や西へむかへば善光寺
na no hana ya nishi e mukaeba zenkōji

flowering mustard—
and looking west
Zenkō Temple

1789

木々おのおの名乗り出たる木の芽哉

kigi ono-ono nanori idetaru ko no me kana

every tree
with its calling card...
spring buds

1823

木々の芽の春さめざめと小鳥鳴く也

kigi no me no haru same-zame to ko tori naku nari

for the budding trees' spring
a little bird
gushes song

1804

雨だれの毎日たたく椿哉

amadare no mainichi tataku tsubaki kana

clobbered every day
by raindrops from the eaves...
camellias

1805

牛の子の顔をつん出す椿哉

ushi no ko no kao wo tsundasu tsubaki kana

a calf's face
stretches forward...
camellias

1813

かまくらや昔どなたの千代椿

kamakura ya mukashi donata no chiyo tsubaki

Kamakura—
who planted these camellias
in olden times?

1815

仰のけに寝てしやぶりけり藤の花

aonoke ni nete shaburi keri fuji no hana

lying on her back
sucking on the dangling
wisteria

Or: "on his back" or "on my back."

1802

片枝は都の空よむめの花
kata eda wa miyako no sora yo mume no hana

one branch makes
Kyoto's sky...
plum blossoms

1803

片枝の待遠しさよ梅の花
kata eda no machi-dōshisa yo ume no hana

waiting so long
for just one branch...
plum blossoms

1803

松間にひとりすまして梅の花
matsu ai ni hitori sumashite ume no hana

among the pines
all alone
a plum tree blooms

1804

うしろからぼろを笑ふよ梅の花
ushiro kara boro wo warau yo ume no hana

behind me
laughter at my rags...
plum blossoms

1804

梅の月牛の尻迄見ゆる也
ume no tsuki ushi no shiri made miyuru nari

plum blossoms, moon
and the rump
of a cow

1804

我庵の貧乏梅の咲にけり
waga io no bimbō ume no saki ni keri

my hut's
down-and-out plum tree
has bloomed!

1805

梅咲くや三文笛も音を出して
ume saku ya san mon fue mo ne wo dashite

plum blossoms—
the sound of a three-penny
flute

1805

蒲焼の香にまけじとや梅の花
kabayaki no ka ni makeji to ya ume no hana

unconquered
by the smell of broiled eels...
plum blossoms

1806

梅がかに鼬もないて通りけり
ume ga ka ni itachi mo naite tōri keri

plum blossom scent—
even the weasel passes
with a song

1807

馬の子の襟する梅の咲にけり

uma no ko no eri suru ume no saki ni keri

for the pony
it's a neck-scratcher...
blooming plum

1810

梅咲や里に広がる江戸虱

ume saku ya sato ni hirogaru edo-jirami

plum blossoms—
spreading into the countryside
lice of Edo

The blossom-viewers of Edo spread out into the countryside,
bringing with them their city lice.

1812

切ござや銭が四五文梅の花

kiri-goza ya zeni ga shi go mon ume no hana

on his scrap of mat
four or five pennies...
plum blossoms

1812

浄はりや梅盗む手が先うつる

jōhari ya ume nusumu te ga mazu utsuru

in hell's mirror
the plum-blossom thief's
reflection

According to Japanese myth, Emma, the judge of hell, has a magic mirror that reflects the sins of all new arrivals to his realm. Issa declares, with a wink, that someone's (his?) plum blossom stealing will be noted in the infernal mirror.

year unknown

梅さくや犬にまたがる金太郎

ume saku ya inu ni matagaru kintarō

plum blossoms—
riding a dog
the Golden Boy

A doll of Kintarō 金太郎 ("Golden Boy") riding a bear is a popular doll for the Boy's Festival of fifth day, Fifth Month. In Japanese folklore Kintarō is a boy-hero, an exaggerated depiction of the Heian Era samurai, Sakata no Kintoki.

year unknown

紅梅や縁にほしたる洗ひ猫

kōbai ya heri ni hoshitaru aria neko

red plum blossoms—
on the porch
the bathed cat dries

1816

蟾どのが何か侍る梅の花

hiki dono ga nannika haberu ume no hana

Sir Toad
on a secret mission...
plum blossoms

1817

梅咲くや現金酒の通帳

ume saku ya genkin-zake no kayoichō

plum blossoms—
in my account book I enter
"cash for sake"

Issa might be (humorously? regretfully?) implying that he has no credit at the local sake shop, having failed to settle the account at the end of the previous year.

1817

不精犬寝て吼る也梅の咲
bushō inu nete hoeru nari ume no saku

the lazy dog
barks lying down...
plum trees in bloom

1817

道の記や一つ月一つ梅の花
michi no ki ya hitotsu tsuki hitotsu ume no hana

travel journal—
one moon
one blooming plum tree

1820

梅咲や地獄の門も休み札
ume saku ya jigoku no kado mo yasumi satsu

plum blooming—
even hell's gate
CLOSED

It is a religious day of fasting in the New Year's season.
Everyone takes the day off.

1818

大馬の尻引こする野梅哉

ōuma no shiri hikkosuru no ume kana

the big horse
rubs his rump...
plum blossoms in the field

1818

子地蔵よ御手出し給へ梅の花

ko jizō yo o-te dashi tamae ume no hana

holy Jizō
stretch forth your hand!
plum blossoms

Jizō is the beloved guardian deity of children. In this haiku, Issa refers to him as *ko jizō* ("child Jizō"). He could be referring to a statue of Jizō as a child, or of one in which the adult bodhisattva is protecting a child.

1819

梅の花ここを盗めとさす月か

ume no hana koko wo nusume to sasu tsuki ka

are you pointing out
these plum blossoms for stealing,
moon?

1820

臭水の井戸の際より梅の花

kusa mizu no ido no kiwa yori ume no hana

at the edge
of a stinking well...
plum blossoms

1820

ひらひらとつむりにしみる梅の花

hira-hira to tsumuri ni shimiru ume no hana

fluttering their way
onto my head...
plum blossoms

In the first edition I chose the more poetic phrase, "into my head." The current version is more literal.

1821

おのづから頭が下る也梅の花

onozukara zu ga sagaru nari ume no hana

by itself
my head bows...
plum blossoms!

1821

在郷や雪隠神も梅の花
zaigō ya setchin-gami mo ume no hana

even for the god
of the outhouse...
plum blossoms

1822

梅咲けど湯桁は水で流れけり
ume sakedo yugeta wa mizu de nagare keri

when plum trees bloom
hot tubs
overflow

1822

雪隠の錠も明く也梅の花
setchin no jō mo aku nari ume no hana

he leaves the outhouse
unlatched...
plum blossoms!

1824

梅さくやごまめちらばふ猫の墓
ume saku ya gomame chirabau neko no haka

plum blossoms—
dried sardines scattered
on the cat's grave

1792

もし降らば天津乙女ぞ花曇
moshi furaba amatsuotome zo hana kumori

have celestial maidens
descended to earth?
blossom clouds

1798

あの鐘の上野に似たり花の雲
ano kane no ueno ni nitari hana no kumo

that temple bell
sounds like Ueno's...
clouds of blossoms

Ueno is a famous place for blossom viewing. Issa is alluding to Bashō's famous haiku, *hana no kumo kane wa ueno ka asakusa ka* 花の雲鐘は上野か浅草か (clouds of blossoms/ is

157

that the bell of Ueno/ or of Asakusa?); Issa's answer: "The bell sounds like Ueno's!"

1803

夕暮や鳥とる鳥の花に来る
yūgure ya tori toru tori no hana ni kuru

evening—
a bird of prey flies home
into blossoms

1804

どこからの花のなぐれぞ角田川
doko kara no hana no nagure zo sumida-gawa

from where
did those blossoms float?
Sumida River

1804

奈良漬を丸でかじりて花の陰
narazuke wo maru de kajirite hana no kage

eating my pickle
rind and all...
blossom shade

1804

ふる雨に一人残りし花の陰
furu ame ni hitori nokorishi hana no kage

in falling rain
one man remains...
blossom shade

1807

咲花やけふをかぎりの江戸住居
saku hana ya kyō wo kagiri no edo sumai

cherry blossoms—
I've been living in Edo
for this day!

1807

花の雨ことしも罪を作りけり
hana no ame kotoshi mo tsumi wo tsukuri keri

rain of cherry blossoms—
this year, too
I've sinned

1808

乞食も一曲あるか花の陰
konjiki mo ikkyoku aru ka hana no kage

is even the beggar
singing a song?
blossom shade

1808

ちる花をざぶざぶ浴る雀哉
chiru hana wo zabu-zabu abiru suzume kana

splish-splash
the sparrow takes
a blossom bath

1809

ただ頼め花ははらはらあの通り
tada tanome hana wa hara-hara ano tōri

simply trust!
cherry blossoms flitting
down

1810

斯う活て居るも不思議ぞ花の陰
kō ikite iru mo fushigi zo hana no kage

to be alive like this
is a wonder...
blossom shade

1810

さく花に長逗留の此世哉
saku hana ni naga-tōryū no kono yo kana

among cherry blossoms
a long stay
in this world

1810

花ちるや称名うなる寺の犬
hana chiru ya shōmyō unaru tera no inu

in falling blossoms
growling to Amida Buddha...
temple dog

1812

さく花の中にうごめく衆生哉

saku hana no naka ni ugomeku shujō kana

squirming
through the cherry blossoms...
people

This haiku is poem five of Issa's six-poem series on the Six Ways. Humans infest the cherry grove, wriggling through it like worms—an unforgettable image that suggests, for Issa, that the essence of human nature is the love of beauty. He also notes, with a wry smile, that humans can tend to mar the beauty they love: during cherry-blossom season droves of people pour into the countryside, "squirming" among the flowers.

1812

世の中は地獄の上の花見哉

yo no naka wa jigoku no ue no hanami kana

in this world
over hell...
gazing at blossoms

This haiku is the first poem of one version of Issa's six-poem series on the Six Ways of Buddhist reincarnation. The present haiku appears only in the original, 1812 version. In it, Issa offers a striking juxtaposition: above, people enjoy a pleasant day of viewing spring blossoms—drinking sake, eating, joking, laughing—while deep below poor souls suffer the torments of hell. The contrast suggests that, for Issa, the opposite of hell isn't heaven; it's being in this world on a glorious spring day. The poem is Issa's one-breath *Divine Comedy.*

1813

ちる花を引つかぶりたる狗哉
chiru hana wo hikkaburitaru enoko kana

tucking himself in
under fallen blossoms
puppy

1813

花の山心の鬼も出てあそべ
hana no yama kokoro no oni mo dete asobe

blossoming mountain—
come out and play
devil in me!

1814

我に似てちり下手なるや門の花

ware ni nite chiri-beta naru ya kado no hana

like me
no good at dying...
blossoms at the gate

1818

散花の辰巳へそれる屁玉哉

chiru hana no tatsu mi e soreru hedama kana

all morning
to the falling blossoms...
my farts

1818

花さくや伊達に加へし空ぎせる

hana saku ya date ni kuwaeshi kara giseru

cherry blossoms—
playing the dandy, in my mouth
an empty pipe

A Japanese advisor, Sakuo Nakamura, explains that this haiku refers to a popular kabuki play, *Shiranami gonin oto-ko* ("White Waves, Five Men" 白波五人男), in which Benten

Kozō, a robber in female dress, says that he is "playing the dandy with a pipe" under the cherry blossoms.

1819

花の陰赤の他人はなかりけり
hana no kage aka no tanin wa nakari keri

cherry blossom shade—
no one an utter
stranger

1820

草庵に来てはこそこそ花見哉
sōan ni kite wa koso-koso hanami kana

he sneaks up
to my thatched hut
for blossom viewing

1820

草庵に来てはくつろぐ花見哉
sōan ni kite wa kutsurogu hanami kana

treating my thatched hut
like home...
blossom viewers

1820

若い衆に先越れしよ花の陰
wakai shu ni saki kosareshi yo hana no kage

young folk beat us
to the spot!
blossom shade

1822

下戸衆はさもいんき也花の陰
geko shū wa samo inki nari hana no kage

all the nondrinkers
seem gloomy...
blossom shade

1822

寺の花はり合もなく散りにけり
tera no hana hariai mo naku chiri ni keri

the temple blossoms
without struggle
fall

1822

花は雲人はかぶりと成にけり

hana wa kumo hito wa keburi to nari ni keri

blossoms become clouds—
people become
smoke

1823

花さくや京の美人の頬かぶり

hana saku ya kyō no bijin no hohokaburi

cherry blossoms—
the pretty women of Kyoto
cheeks wrapped in scarves

Literally, the pretty women of Kyoto tie cloths around their cheeks, peasant-style.

1824

江戸声や花見の果のけん嘩かひ

edo-goe ya hanami no hate no kenka kai

Edo voices—
the blossom viewing ends
in a quarrel

1824

上下の酔倒あり花の陰
kamishimo no yoidaore ari hana no kage

in ceremonial robe
he's fallen down drunk...
blossom shade

The sake flowed freely at cherry blossom viewing parties.

year unknown

声々に花の木蔭のばくち哉
koe-goe ni hana no kokage no bakuchi kana

fussing, fussing
in the blossom shade...
gamblers

This haiku is poem four of Issa's six-poem series on the Six Ways of Buddhist reincarnation. Issa thus poetically associates gamblers with angry demons. The present haiku appears only in the posthumously published 1829 version.

year unknown

親負て子の手を引いてさくら哉

oya oute ko no te wo hiite sakura kana

carrying his mother
and leading his child by the hand...
cherry blossoms!

year unknown

軍勢甲乙入べからずとさくら哉

gunzei kō-otsu iri-bekarazu to sakura kana

"No soldiers
allowed!"
say the cherry blossoms

year unknown

見かぎりし古郷の桜咲にけり

mikagirishi furusato no sakura saki ni keri

the home village
I abandoned...
cherry trees in bloom

This haiku has the headnote, "Third Month, twentieth day, entering Kashiwabara." Kashiwabara was Issa's native village. From his early teens up to his fifties Issa "abandoned"

Kashiwabara.

1804

大川へ吹なぐられし桜哉

ōkawa e fuki nagurareshi sakura kana

blown to the big river
floating away...
cherry blossoms

1805

米袋空しくなれど桜哉

kome-bukuro munashiku naredo sakura kana

though my rice sack
is empty...
cherry blossoms!

1806

姥捨し片山桜咲にけり

ubasuteshi kata yama-zakura saki ni keri

on Mount Ubasute
where the old were left to die...
cherry blossoms

1806

夕過や桜の下に小言いふ
yū sugi ya sakura no shita ni kogoto yū

all night
under the cherry blossoms
nagging

1808

花咲くや桜が下のばくち小屋
hana saku ya sakura ga shita no bakuchi-goya

under the cherry tree
in bloom
a little gambling shack

1809

つくづくと蛙が目にも桜哉
tsukuzuku to kawazu ga me ni mo sakura kana

even the frog's eyes
can't turn away...
cherry blossoms!

1810

狗が供して参る桜かな

enokoro ga tomo shite mairu sakura kana

the puppy is escort
on the pilgrimage...
cherry blossoms!

1810

鬼の角ぽつきり折るる桜哉

oni no tsuno pokkiri oruru sakura kana

the devil's horns
snap off!
cherry blossoms

1811

家根をはく人の立けり夕桜

yane wo haku hito no tachi keri yūzakura

the roof sweeper
stands still...
evening cherry blossoms

1813

ちる桜犬に詫して通りけり
chiru sakura inu ni wabishite tōri keri

the cherry blossoms fall—
I apologize to a dog
in passing

1814

気に入た桜の蔭もなかりけり
ki ni itta sakura no kage mo nakari keri

the cherry blossoms
that stirred me, shade me
no more

1814

迷子のしつかり掴むさくら哉
mayoigo no shikkari tsukamu sakura kana

the lost child
clutches them tightly...
cherry blossoms

1814

みちのくの鬼住里も桜かな
michi no ku no oni sumu sato mo sakura kana

remote province—
even in a haunted place
cherry blossoms

1814

山桜花の主や石仏
yamazakura hana no aruji ya ishi-botoke

lord of the mountain's
cherry blossoms...
stone Buddha

1815

日本は這入口からさくらかな
nippon wa hairiguchi kara sakura kana

from Japan's
front door on...
cherry blossoms!

1815

湯も浴て仏おがんで桜かな
yu mo abite hotoke ogande sakura kana

a hot bath
a prayer
then cherry blossoms!

1816

なむなむと桜明りに寝たりけり
namu namu to sakura akari ni netari keri

praise Buddha!
sleeping in the light
of cherry blossoms

1822

婆々どのも牛に引かれて桜かな
baba dono mo ushi ni hikarete sakura kana

granny comes too
led by a cow...
cherry blossoms

1824

飴ン棒にべつたり付し桜哉

amenbō ni bettari tsukishi sakura kana

sticking to
her stick of candy...
cherry blossoms

Or: "his stick of candy" or "my stick of candy."

1824

大名を馬からおろす桜哉

daimyō wo uma kara orosu sakura kana

the war lord
forced off his horse...
cherry blossoms

Though this haiku has the headnote, "Ueno" 上野, it was composed in Shinano Province during a snowy Second Month in 1824. At the foot of Ueno hill, a "Dismount Your Horse" placard was posted; Maruyama Kazuhiko, *Issa haiku shū* 344.

year unknown

君なくて誠に多太の桜哉

kimi nakute makoto ni tada no sakura kana

without you—
the cherry blossoms
just blossoms

year unknown

里の子の袂からちる桜かな

sato no ko no tamoto kara chiru sakura kana

trickling from
a village child's sleeve...
cherry blossoms

year unknown

欲面へ浴せかけたる桜哉

yoku tsura e abise-kaketaru sakura kana

pouring onto
the faces of sinners...
cherry blossoms

1804

福蟾ものさばり出たり桃の花
fuku-biki mo nosabari detari momo no hana

Lucky the Toad, too
swaggers out...
peach blossoms

1825

立午の尻こする也桃の花
tatsu uma no shiri kosuru nari momo no hana

the horse stands
rubbing his rump...
peach blossoms

1812

山吹にぶらりと牛のふぐり哉
yamabuki ni burari to ushi no fuguri kana

dangling
in the yellow roses
the bull's balls

1802

薄月の礎しめる柳哉

usu-zuki no ishizue shimeru yanagi kana

holding up
the hazy moon...
willow tree

1804

蛍よぶ夜のれうとやさし柳

hotaru yobu yoru no ryō to ya sashi yanagi

an evening spot
for calling fireflies...
planting a willow

Issa is visualizing the future. When the willow is large and shady, people will sit under it in the summertime, calling fireflies.

1805

朝やけも又めづらしき柳哉

asayake mo mata mezurashiki yanagi kana

dawn's glow
even more of a wonder...
willow tree

1806

夕山に肩を並ぶる柳哉

yū yama ni kata wo naraburu yanagi kana

lined up
with the evening mountain...
a willow

1808

鶏〆る門の柳の青みけり

tori shimeru kado no yanagi no aomi keri

killing a chicken—
the willow at the gate
so green

1813

柳からももんぐわとて出る子哉

yanagi kara momonguwa tote deru ko kana

from the willow
a ghost attacks!
the child

The child has thrown a coat over his head and is running out from the shadow of the willow, attempting to scare people (*IZ* 6.171). *Momonguwa* is another word for the Japanese flying squirrel (*musasabi*); more generally it refers to a wide-eyed, mouth-open boogieman who frightens children; see *KDJ* 1642.

year unknown
犬の子の踏まへて眠る柳哉
inu no ko no fumaete nemuru yanagi kana

the sleeping puppy
paws
at the willow

1819
野雪隠のうしろをかこふ柳哉
no setchin no ushiro wo kakou yanagi kana

shrouding his rear
as he poops in the field...
a willow

1819
一吹にほんの柳と成にけり
hito fuki ni hon no yanagi to nari ni keri

with one gust
it becomes the perfect
willow

181

1820

馬の子が柳潜りをしたりけり
uma no ko ga yanagi kuguri wo shitari keri

the pony
has crept
through the willow

1823

夜に入れば遊女袖引く柳哉
yo ni ireba yūjo sode hiku yanagi kana

when night falls
whores tug at sleeves...
willow tree

The expression, *sode hiku* 袖引く literally denotes dragging
one by the sleeve; metaphorically, it refers to seduction.

year unknown

洗たくの婆々へ柳の夕なびき
sentaku no baba e yanagi no yū nabiki

to the old woman
doing laundry, the evening
willow bows

year unknown

水まして蝦這のぼる柳哉

mizu mashite ebi hai-noboru yanagi kana

water rising—
the shrimp crawls up
the willow

For Issa the word *ebi* 蝦 would have denoted both marine and freshwater varieties: shrimp and crayfish.

柳からまねまね出たり狐面

yanagi kara mane-mane detari kitsune tsura

peeking out
from the willow tree...
face of a fox

1811

ゆさゆさと春が行ぞよのべの草

yusa-yusa to haru ga yuku zo yo nobe no kusa

swish-swish
spring is departing...
field of grass

6. SUMMER

1794

夏の暁や牛に寝てゆく秣刈

ge no ake ya ushi ni nete yuku magusa kari

summer dawn—
riding an ox, asleep
the hay cutter

1808

短夜を継たしてなく蛙哉

mijika yo wo tsugitashite naku kawazu kana

stitching together
the short summer nights...
croaking frogs

1813

短夜やくねり盛の女郎花

mijika yo ya kuneri-zakari no ominaeshi

in the short summer night
wriggling to climax...
maiden flowers

Issa is playing with the flower's name (*ominaeshi* 女郎花: "maiden flower") and a sexual double-entendre.

1814

明安き夜を触歩く雀哉

akeyasuki yo wo fure-aruku suzume kana

"Dawn's coming quick!"
cries the town crier...
sparrow

The seasonal reference of this haiku is to the short nights of summer.

1825

短夜の畠に亀のあそび哉

mijika yo no hatake ni kame no asobi kana

short summer night—
in the field turtles
cavort

1815

暑き夜をにらみ合たり鬼瓦

atsuki yo wo nirami aitari onigawara

scowling
at the hot night...
gargoyle

1818

暑き日やひやと算盤枕哉

atsuki hi ya hiya to soroban makura kana

hot day—
the cool abacus
for a pillow

This haiku has the headnote, "Dog days [of midsummer] at a shop."

1819

あついとてつらで手習した子かな

atsui tote tsura de tenari shita ko kana

ink-stained hands
sweaty face...
the child's calligraphy!

The editors of *Issa zenshū* comment, "A sweaty face has been rubbed with ink-covered hands" (6.142). The child becomes art.

1819

暑き夜や蝙蝠かける川ばたに
atsuki yo ya kōmori kakeru kawa-bata ni

hot night—
bats dangle
at the river's edge

1824

暑き日やにらみくらする鬼瓦
atsuki hi ya niramikura suru onigawara

hot day—
a staring contest with
a gargoyle

1794

涼しさや半月うごく溜まり水
suzushisa ya hangetsu ugoku tamarimizu

cool air—
the half moon moves
across a puddle

Or: "across puddles."

1808

とくとくと水の涼しや蜂の留守
toku-toku to mizu no suzushi ya hachi no rusu

drip-drip
goes cool water...
bees have left their hive

1810

涼しさや闇の隅なる角田川
suzushisa ya yami no sumi naru sumida-gawa

cool air—
a dark little nook
on Sumida River

1811

涼しさにぶらぶら地獄巡り哉
suzushisa ni bura-bura jigoku meguri kana

in summer cool
ambling down my road
to hell

Sakuo Nakamura imagines that this haiku is about a visit to a hot spring located at the bottom of a valley. But if Issa literally means that he is on the path to hell, this calls to mind the teaching of Shinran, the Pure Land Buddhist patriarch who argued that sin is inevitable, and therefore one should cultivate a spiritual attitude of trustful non-striving to achieve enlightenment.

1811

涼しさは雲の作りし仏哉
suzushisa wa kumo no tsukurishi hotoke kana

cool air—
the shape of the cloud
is Buddha

1813

下々も下々下々の下国の涼しさよ
gege mo gege gege no gegoku no suzushisa yo

it's a down, down
downtrodden land...
but cool!

Issa is most likely referring to his impoverished home province of Shinano.

1813

大の字に寝て涼しさよ淋しさよ

dai no ji ni nete suzushisa yo sabishisa yo

lying spread-eagle
cool
lonely

With arms and legs spread wide, the poet's body forms the Japanese character "big" (大).

1814

涼風の第一番は後架也

suzukaze no dai ichi ban wa kōka nari

the number one
best cool breeze...
outhouse

1814

夕涼や水投つける馬の尻

yūsuzu ya mizu nage-tsukeru uma no shiri

evening cool—
tossing water on the
horse's rump

1825

涼しさや汁の椀にも不二の山
suzushisa ya shiru no wan ni mo fuji no yama

cool air—
even in my soup bowl
Mount Fuji!

1819

涼しさにしやんと髪結御馬哉
suzushisa ni shan to kamiyuu o-uma kana

in the cool air
slap! slap! his hair is combed...
Sir Horse

1819

涼しさに大福帳を枕かな
suzushisa ni daifukuchō wo makura kana

in summer cool
the account book
for a pillow

1819

涼しさや極楽浄土の這入口
suzushisa ya goraku jōdo no hairiguchi

summer cool—
the gate to Buddha's
Pure Land

Issa imagines the Western Paradise—symbolic of enlighten-
ment—to be in this world or at least right next door to it.
Nature perceived with open heart and mind is the gateway.

1822

涼風や何喰はせても二人前
suzukaze ya nani kuwasete mo ni nin mae

cool breeze—
she eats with an appetite
for two

This haiku has the headnote, "Congratulating my woman
Kiku." Issa's wife had recovered from an illness and, to his
joy, regained her appetite.

1823

涼しさや夜水のかかる井戸の音
suzushisa ya yo mizu no kakaru ido no oto

cool air—
the sound of well water
drawn at night

1824

涼しさは直に神代の木立哉
suzushisa wa sugu ni kamiyo no kodachi kana

cool air—
straight from the holy grove
it comes

Issa is referring to a grove in the precincts of a Shinto shrine.
The cool air seems a blessing from the god(s).

1825

涼しさや切紙の雪はらはらと
suzushisa ya kirigami no yuki hara-hara to

cool air—
paper snowflakes fluttering
down

year unknown
涼しさは蚊を追ふ妹が杓子哉
suzushisa wa ka wo ou imo ga shakushi kana

cool air—
my wife chases a mosquito
with a spoon

1814
鬼と成り仏となるや土用雲
oni to nari hotoke to naru ya doyōgumo

becoming demons
becoming Buddhas...
the midsummer clouds

1823
此雨は天から土用見廻かな
kono ame wa ten kara doyō mimai kana

this rain
a greeting card from heaven...
midsummer heat

1823

吹風も土用休みか草の原
fuku kaze mo doyō yasumi ka kusa no hara

is the wind
on summer vacation?
grassy field

1817

入梅や蟹かけ歩大座敷
nyūbai ya kani kake-aruku ōzashiki

rainy season—
a crab strolls into
the big sitting room

1804

けふも暮けふも暮けり五月雨
kyō mo kure kyō mo kure keri satsuki ame

all day, all day
day after day...
Fifth Month rain

"Fifth Month rain" (*samidare* 五月雨) pertains to the old lunar calendar; it would be June rain in the present calendar.

195

1804

二人とは行かれぬ厨子や五月雨
futari towa ikarenu zushi ya satsuki ame

two won't fit
in the little shrine…
Fifth Month rain

1805

五月雨におつぴしげたる住居哉
samidare ni oppishigetaru sumai kana

crushed
under the Fifth Month rain…
my home

1812

五月雨つつじをもたぬ石もなし
samidare tsutsuji wo motanu ishi mo nashi

Fifth Month rain—
not a rock
without azaleas

1814

五月雨に さくさく歩く烏かな

samidare ni saku-saku aruku karasu kana

in Fifth Month rain
splish-splash the strutting
crow

1816

薮陰やひとり鎌とぐ五月雨

yabu kage ya hitori kama togu satsuki ame

in the thicket shade
he sharpens his sickle...
Fifth Month rain

1818

ひきどのの仏頂面や五月雨

hiki dono no butchōzura ya satsuki ame

Mr. Toad's
sour Buddha face...
Fifth Month rain

1818

面壁の三介どのや五月雨

mempeki no sansuke dono ya satsuki ame

a servant in Zen meditation
faces a wall...
Fifth Month rain

1821

なぐさみに風呂に入也五月雨

nagusami ni furo ni iru nari satsuki ame

just for fun
into the hot tub I go...
Fifth Month rain

1821

何の其蛙の面や五月雨

nanno sono kawazu no tsura ya satsuki ame

what a face
this frog is making!
Fifth Month rain

year unknown

朝顔に翌なる蔓や五月雨

asagao ni asu naru tsuru ya satsuki ame

vines today
morning-glories tomorrow...
Fifth Month rain

1816

蛇出よせうじの破の五月晴

abu ide yo shōji no yare no satsuki-bare

go, horsefly
through the ripped paper door!
Fifth Month rains are over

year unknown

夕立や乞食どのの鉢の松

yūdachi ya kojiki dono no hachi no matsu

rainstorm—
a beggar with his potted
pine

1812

夕立やかみつくやうな鬼瓦

yūdachi ya kamitsuku yōna onigawara

like he's snapping
at the downpour...
gargoyle

1814

夕立は是切とぱらりぱらり哉

yūdachi wa koregiri to parari parari kana

now the cloudburst
only a pitter
patter

1815

夕立を鐘の下から見たりけり

yūdachi wo kane no shita kara mitari keri

watching the downpour
from under a temple
bell

1818

夕立に拍子を付る乙鳥哉

yūdachi ni hyōshi wo tsukeru tsubame kana

darting to the beat
of the downpour...
a swallow

1821

夕立の真中に立座頭かな

yūdachi no mannaka ni tatsu zatō kana

standing dead center
in the downpour...
a blind man

1825

夕立や裸で乗しはだか馬

yūdachi ya hadaka de norishi hadaka uma

rainstorm—
a naked rider
on a naked horse

1792

しづかさや湖水の底の雲のみね

shizukasa ya kosui no soko no kumo no mine

stillness—
in the depths of the lake
billowing clouds

1803

雲の峰いささか松が退くか

kumo no mine isasaka matsu ga shirizoku ka

billowing clouds—
have the pine trees
shrunk a bit?

1804

虫のなる腹をさぐれば雲の峰

mushi no naru hara wo sagureba kumo no mine

patting my belly
full of worms...
billowing clouds

Or: "his belly" or "her belly." Issa suggests that rain will fall from the clouds and cause crops to grow, thus making food. For now, he pats his hungry (and worm-filled) belly...and waits.

1813

水およぐ蚤の思ひや雲の峰
mizu oyogu nomi no omoi ya kumo no mine

the swimming flea
thinks to reach them...
billowing clouds

1819

蟻の道雲の峰よりつづきけり
ari no michi kumo no mine yori tsuzuki keri

the ants' road
from billowing clouds
to here

1826

人のなす罪より低し雲の峰
hito no nasu tsumi yori hikushi kumo no mine

less high
than the sins of men...
billowing clouds

1804

汁なべも厠も夏の月よ哉

shiru nabe mo kawaya mo natsu no tsuki yo kana

in soup kettle
and outhouse
the summer moon

1803

夏山や一足づつに海見ゆる

natsu yama ya hito ashi zutsu ni umi miyuru

summer mountain—
with each step more
of the sea

1808

蜂の巣のてくてく下る清水哉

hachi no su no teku-teku sagaru shimizu kana

the beehive dangles
heavily above...
pure water

1815

毒草の花の陰より清水哉
dokusō no hana no kage yori shimizu kana

from the shade
of the poison plant...
pure water

1822

人里へ出れば清水でなかりけり
hito-zato e dereba shimizu de nakari keri

through a village of people
the water no longer
pure

1810

夕陰や清水を馬に投つける
yūkage ya shimizu wo uma ni nagetsukeru

evening shadows—
he throws pure water
on the horse

姫ゆりの心ありげの清水哉
himeyuri no kokoro arige no shimizu kana

touching the princess lily's
heart...
pure water

青田原箸とりながら見たりけり
aodabara hashi tori nagara mitari keri

green rice field—
grabbing the chopsticks
he watches

This is an early haiku written in the 1790s. Thinking way ahead to harvest time, the farmer (and/or Issa) can almost taste the grain to come.

1801

父ありて明ぼの見たし青田原
chichi arite akebono mitashi aodabara

if my father were here—
dawn colors
over green fields

This haiku appears at the end of *Chichi no shūen nikki* ("The Journal of My Father's Last Days"), a journal in which Issa narrates the death of his father.

1806

手枕におのが青田と思ふ哉

temakura ni ono ga aoda to omou kana

an arm for a pillow
imagining the green rice field
is mine

1815

君が田も我田も同じ青み哉

kimi ga ta mo waga ta mo onaji aomi kana

your rice field
my rice field
the same green

1827

夕飯の膳の際より青田哉

yūmeshi no zen no kiwa yori aoda kana

at the dinner
tray's edge...
a green rice field

1806

灌仏やふくら雀も親連れて
kanbutsu ya fukura suzume mo oya tsurete

Buddha's birthday—
fat little sparrows
and their parents

On the eighth day of Fourth Month Gautama Buddha's birthday is celebrated.

1818

御仏や乞食町にも御誕生
mi-hotoke ya kojiki-chō ni mo o-tanjō

the Buddha
even in beggar-town
is born

1821

虻蜂の大吉日や花御堂
abu hachi no ōkichi nichi ya hanamidō

horseflies' and bees'
big lucky day...
Buddha's birthday flowers

1821

蟻の道はや付にけり花御堂

ari no michi haya tsuki ni keri hanamidō

the ants rush
to make a road...
Buddha's birthday flowers

1825

夏籠や毎晩見舞ふ引がへる

ge-gomori ya maiban mimau hikigaeru

summer seclusion—
every night the toad
comes calling

year unknown

かたつぶりそろそろ登れ富士の山

katatsuburi soro-soro nobore fuji no yama

little snail
inch by inch, climb
Mount Fuji!

In Issa's time, climbing Mount Fuji was thought to be a
sacred pilgrimage. However, not everyone could make the
climb. Therefore, imitation Mount Fujis (small, sculpted hills)

were built at various temples and shrines so that everyone, including the infirm and elderly, could reap spiritual benefit by climbing them. Issa's snail is climbing one of these pseudo-mountains. Its climb has both Shinto and Buddhist significance. For Shinto, Mount Fuji is the home of the great goddess Konohanasakuya-hime, enshrined near the summit. For Buddhists, it is the abode of Dainichi Nyorai 大日如来, the Buddha of All-Illuminating Wisdom, and its snowy peak represents a supreme state of meditative concentration or *zenjō* 禅定. The snail climbs to the goddess's blessing; the snail climbs to enlightenment.

1803

えた町に見おとされたる幟哉
eta machi ni miotosaretaru nobori kana

in the outcastes' village
easily overlooked...
summer banners

1820

御地蔵のお首にかけるちまき哉
o-jizō no o-kubi ni kakeru chimaki kana

from holy Jizō's
holy neck it hangs...
rice dumpling

Rice dumplings (*chimaki* ちまき) are wrapped in bamboo grass. Here, someone has left one as an offering to the bodhisattva Jizō.

1821

小坊主の首にかけたる粽かな
ko bōzu no kubi ni kaketaru chimaki kana

dangling from
the little boy's neck...
a rice dumpling

The "little priest" (*ko bōzu* 小坊主) in this haiku might signify not only a Buddhist acolyte but any small, smooth-headed boy.

1821

猫の子のほどく手つきや笹粽
neko no ko no hodoku tetsuki ya sasa chimaki

the kitten unwraps it
with clever paws...
rice dumpling

1814

蜻蛉も起てはたらく夜川哉
tombō mo okite hataraku yo kawa kana

the dragonfly, too
works late...
night fishing

1816

叱られて又疲うの入にけり
shikararete mata tsukare u no iri ni keri

after a scolding
the weary cormorants
dive again

Japanese fishermen use cormorants. Tied to a tether, these sea birds dive for fish that they are forced to disgorge. In this case, the birds have come up empty-beaked only to be scolded by their handler and thrown back into the water.

1817

一村やうにかせがせて夕枕
hito mura ya u ni kasegasete yūmakura

the whole town sleeps
while the cormorants
toil

1819

鵜の真似を鵜より巧者な子供哉
u no mane wo u yori kōsha-na kodomo kana

outdoing the cormorant
in skillful imitation...
a child

year unknown

つかれ鵜の節句やすみもなかりけり
tsukare u no sekku yasumi mo nakari keri

weary cormorant—
no festival holiday
for you

1821

今日も今日も今日も今日もやだまし雲
kyō mo kyō mo kyō mo kyō mo ya damashi kumo

today too
today too...
cheating clouds

This haiku has the headnote, "Praying for Rain."

1813

牛馬の汗の玉ちる草葉哉

ushi uma no ase no tama chiru kusaba kana

sweat drops from cows
from horses...
blades of grass

1795

衣がえ替ても旅のしらみ哉

koromogae kaete mo tabi no shirami kana

also changing
into a summer robe...
my journey's lice

In this comic haiku, Issa changes into a summer robe on the first day of summer—the first day of Fourth Month in the old Japanese calendar. His body lice have changed clothes too.

1810

何をして腹をへらさん更衣

nani wo shite hara wo herasan koromogae

doing what I can
to shrink the belly...
new summer robe

1814

蒲公英は天窓そりけり更衣
tanpopo wa atama sori keri koromogae

the dandelion gives
a nod...
my new summer robe

1816

けふばかり隣ほしさよ更衣
kyō bakari tonari hoshisa yo koromogae

just today
I wish I had neighbors...
my new summer robe

1817

誰か又我死がらで更衣
dare ka mata waga shinigara de koromogae

when I'm dead
who'll wear it next?
new summer robe

1824

親の親の其のおやののを更衣
oya no oya no sono oya no no wo koromogae

his father's
father's father wore it too...
summer robe

1814

泣虫と云れてもなく袷哉
naki mushi to iwarete mo naku awase kana

called a crybaby
she starts crying...
summer kimono

1804

僧正が野糞遊ばす日傘哉
sōjō ga no-guso asobasu higasa kana

the high priest
poops in the field...
parasol

Issa is often bold and iconoclastic—poetically and politically.
He doesn't hesitate to poke fun at authority, in this case,
portraying the high priest of a Buddhist temple in a moment

that isn't exactly flattering. The priest does his business outside, shaded by a parasol—most likely being held by an acolyte.

1822

老僧の草引むしる日傘かな
rōsō no kusa hiki-mushiru higasa kana

old priest—
even while plucking grass
a parasol holder

1824

塗盆に猫の寝にけり夏座敷
nuribon ni neko no ne ni keri natsu zashiki

the cat naps
in a lacquered tray...
summer room

1809

蚊屋の穴かぞへ留りや三ケの月
kaya no ana kazoe tomari ya mika no tsuki

stopping to count
my mosquito net's holes...
sickle moon

The moon is a "three-day moon" (*mika no tsuki* 三ケの月) ...just a sliver. As a humorous touch, the moon seems to be doing the counting.

1819

今迄は罰もあたらず昼寝蚊屋
ima made wa bachi mo atarazu hirune kaya

no divine punishment yet—
napping
under the net

1820

新しき蚊屋に寝る也江戸の馬
atarashiki kaya ni neru nari edo no uma

sleeping under
new mosquito nets...
horses of Edo

year unknown

翌日も翌同じ夕べや独り蚊屋
asu mo asu onaji yūbe ya hitori kaya

tomorrow night and the next
the same...
in my mosquito net, alone

1815

逢坂や荷牛の上に一昼寝
ausaka ya ni ushi no ue ni hito hirune

Osaka—
on the back of an ox
a siesta

1818

大の字にふんばたがつて昼寝哉
dai no ji ni funbatagatte hirune kana

spread-eagle arms
legs opened wide...
siesta

year unknown

人並に猿もごろりと昼寝哉
hito nami ni saru mo gorori to hirune kana

like the humans
a monkey too
curled up for siesta

1807

此月に扇かぶつて寝たりけり
kono tsuki ni ōgi kabutte netari keri

such a moon!
yet he's under his fan
asleep

1815

闇がりにひらりひらりと扇哉
kuragari ni hirari-hirari to ōgi kana

in the darkness
swishing, swishing...
paper fan

1818

小うたひの尻べたたたく扇哉
ko utai no shiribeta tataku ōgi kana

singing a song
and slapping his butt...
with a fan

1819

小道者や手を引れつつ赤扇
ko dōsha ya te wo hitaretsutsu aka ōgi

the little pilgrim
being led by hand...
red paper fan

Visiting a Buddhist temple or Shinto shrine accompanied by
a parent, the child holds a red paper fan.

1820

ていねいに鼠の喰し扇かな
teinei ni nezumi no kuishi ōgi kana

top to bottom
the mouse eats
the fan

1805

反故団扇しやにかまへたるひとり哉
hogo uchiwa sha ni kamaetaru hitori kana

with my wastepaper fan
striking poses...
alone

1809

宵々や団扇とるさへむつかしき
yoi-yoi ya uchiwa toru sae mutsukashiki

stroke victim—
even holding a paper fan
an ordeal

1816

大猫のどさりと寝たる団扇哉
ōneko no dosari to netaru uchiwa kana

the big cat
flops down to sleep
on the fan

1817

天から下りた顔して団扇哉
ten kara orita kao shite uchiwa kana

with a face
come down from heaven
she is fanning

1824

寝咄の切間切間を団扇哉

ne-banashi no kirema kirema wo uchiwa kana

in the pauses
of our pillow talk
fanning

Or: "their pillow talk." Shinji Ogawa interprets *ne-banashi* 寝咄 ("sleep talk") as "pillow talk."

1809

蚊いぶしにやがて蛍も去りにけり

ka ibushi ni yagate hotaru mo sari ni keri

smoking out mosquitoes—
soon the fireflies
are gone too

1822

かけ声を井戸の底からこたへけり

kakegoe wo ido no soko kara kotae keri

calling down—
from deep in the well
an answer

Issa refers to the summer custom of draining and cleaning

223

wells.

1822

はやり唄井戸の底から付にけり

hayari uta ido no soko kara tsuke ni keri

a popular song—
from the bottom of the well
he joins in

1805

夜涼や蟾が出ても福といふ

yo suzumi ya hiki ga idete mo fuku to iu

evening cool—
the toad who comes out
I call "Lucky"

1812

煤くさき弥陀と並んで夕涼

susu kusaki mida to narande yūsuzumi

a soot-grimed Amida Buddha
at my side...
evening cool

1814

薮むらや貧乏馴て夕すずみ

yabu mura ya bimbō narete yūsuzumi

in a remote village
they're used to poverty...
evening cool

1815

翌しらぬ盥の魚や夕涼

asu shiranu tarai no uo ya yūsuzumi

the fish in the tub
won't know tomorrow...
evening cool

1815

妻なしが草を咲かせて夕涼

tsuma nashi ga kusa wo sakasete yūsuzumi

a wifeless man
makes his plants bloom...
evening cool

1815

屁くらべや夕顔棚の下涼み
he kurabe ya yūgao-dana no shita suzumi

a farting contest
under the moonflower trellis...
cool air

1815

庖丁で鰻よりつつ夕すずみ
hōchō de unagi yoritsutsu yūsuzumi

with a kitchen knife
choosing eels...
a cool evening

1815

松瘤で肩たたきつつ夕涼
matsu kobu de kata tataki tsutsu yūsuzumi

massaging my back
with the pine tree's gnarl...
evening cool

"Massage" here is hard, Japanese-style pounding (*tataki* たた
き).

year unknown

夜涼や足でかぞへるしなの山

yo suzumi ya ashi de kazoeru shinano yama

evening cool—
with my feet counting
the mountains of Shinano

1815

夜涼みやにらみ合たる鬼瓦

yo suzumi ya nirami autaru onigawara

scowling
at the cool night...
gargoyle

1816

わんぱくや縛れながら夕涼

wanpaku ya shibarare nagara yūsuzumi

naughty child
though tethered enjoys
evening's cool

Tying a child to a tree was a "time out" in Issa's Japan.

1818

大海を手ですくひつつ夕涼

dai umi wo te de sukui tsutsu yūsuzumi

scooping up the ocean
in my hands...
evening cool

1819

線香の火でたばこ吹くすすみかな

senkō no hi de tabako fuku suzumi kana

lighting my pipe
with an incense stick...
cool air

1819

なぐさみに鰐口ならす涼み哉

nagusami ni waniguchi narasu suzumi kana

banging the temple gong
just for fun...
cool air

Waniguchi 鰐口 ("crocodile's mouth") is a metal gong which hangs under the roof of a temple to let priests know that their meals are ready, or for visitors to hit to inform the priests of their presence.

1821

蚊一ッ馬の腹にて涼みけり
abu hitotsu uma no hara nite suzumi keri

one horsefly
on the horse's belly
cooling off

1822

夜涼みや大僧正のおどけ口
yo suzumi ya ōsōjō no odoke kuchi

evening cool—
the great high priest
tells jokes

1824

親と子が屁くらべす也門涼み
oya to ko ga he kurabesu nari kado suzumi

father and son's
fart contest...
cool air at the gate

1814

木がくれや大念仏で田を植る

kogakure ya ōnembutsu de ta wo ueru

hidden in trees
praising Amida Buddha...
rice planter

1815

おれが田も唄の序に植りけり

ore ga ta mo uta no tsuide ni uwari keri

my rice field too
song by song
is planted

1819

おのが里仕廻ふてどこへ田植笠

ono ga sato shimaute doko e taue-gasa

when your village is done
where next?
rice-planting umbrella-hat

This haiku has the headnote, "Feeling pity for a widow alone in the world."

1822

むだな身も呼び出されけり田植酒
mudana mi mo yobidasare keri taue sake

even worthless me
is invited...
rice-planting sake

Issa may be alluding to the fact that he has not participated in the rice planting. Nevertheless, he's invited to partake of the sake.

1825

負ふた子も拍子を泣や田植唄
outa ko mo hyōshi wo naku ya taue uta

the child on her back
cries to the beat...
rice-planting song

1824

早乙女におぶさつて寝る小てふ哉
saotome ni obusatte neru ko chō kana

rice-planting girl—
on her back a butterfly
sleeps

1809

萩の葉と一所に伸びるかのこ哉

hagi no ha to issho ni nobiru kanoko kana

growing up
with the bush clover...
a fawn

1810

弓提し人の跡おふかのこ哉

yumi sageshi hito no ato ou kanoko kana

following behind
the hunter with his bow...
a fawn

1822

鶏にまぶれて育つ鹿の子哉

niwatori ni fumarete sodatsu ka no ko kana

growing up
in the thick of chickens...
a fawn

かはほりよ行々京の飯時分
kawahori yo yuke-yuke kyō no meshi jibun

get a move on, bat!
it's dinnertime
in Kyoto

1817

門の月蚊を喰ふ鳥が時得たり
kado no tsuki ka wo kuu tori ga toki etari

moon at the gate—
the mosquito-eating bats
prosper

Literally, Issa writes, "mosquito-eating birds"—a euphemism for bats.

1824

かはほりに夜ほちもそろりそろり哉
kawahori ni yahochi mo sorori-sorori kana

like the bats
night's streetwalkers too
make their slow rounds

Yahochi 夜ほち is another word for *yotaka* よたか, "nighthawk": a street prostitute. In this and a few other haiku of 1824, Issa makes a playful connection between these night "birds" and bats.

1824

かはほりや仁王の腕にぶら下り
kawahori ya niō no ude ni burasagari

from the arms
of the Deva Kings
bats dangle

Two fierce Deva Kings (*niō* 仁王) stand guard at a temple gate.

1825

かはほりの代々土蔵住居哉
kawahori no dai-dai dozō sumai kana

generations of bats
have called this storehouse
home

1825

洪水やかはほり下る渡し綱
kōzui ya kawahori sagaru watashi-zuna

flood waters—
bats dangle
from the crossing-rope

1795

暁や鶏なき里の時鳥
akatsuki ya tori naki sato no hototogisu

daybreak—
the rooster-less village
has a cuckoo!

1810

我汝を待こと久し時鳥
ware nanji wo matsu koto hisashi hototogisu

I've waited long
for thee
O cuckoo!

This haiku was composed in Fourth Month, 1810. Later, Issa recopied it with explanatory headnotes: "A painting of an old man sitting on a rock handing over a scroll" and "The place where an old man sitting on a rock handed over a scroll"; *IZ* 3.472; 6.152). According to historical tradition, Kōsekikō met Chōryō at Kahi Bridge, where the former conferred upon the latter a scroll containing his tactics of war. Chōryō arrived late, and was greeted by the old man with the words, "I've waited long for thee!" Issa humorously applies this famous quote to his own long wait to hear the song of the cuckoo.

1811

こんな夜は唐にもあろか時鳥
konna yo wa kara ni mo aro ka hototogisu

is the night this nice
in China?
cuckoo

1811

時鳥橋の乞食も聞れけり
hototogisu hashi no kojiki mo kikare keri

a cuckoo—
the bridge beggar
listens too

1812

それでこそ御時鳥松の月

sore de koso on-hototogisu matsu no tsuki

worthy of Sir Cuckoo—
the moon
in the pine

1813

江戸の雨何石呑んだ時鳥

edo no ame nan goku nonda hototogisu

how many gallons
of Edo's rain did you drink?
cuckoo

1814

参詣のたばこにむせな雀の子

sankei no tabako ni musena suzume no ko

temple visit—
don't choke on the pipe smoke
baby sparrow!

1813

我庵は目に這入ぬかほととぎす

waga io wa me ni hairanu ka hototogisu

are you trying not to
look at my hut?
cuckoo

Issa humorously implies that his hut, which he often calls "trashy," is an eyesore—beneath the dignity of the cuckoo to look at.

1815

貧乏雨とは云もののほととぎす

bimbō ame to wa iu mono no hototogisu

"That's a poor excuse
for rain!"
sings the cuckoo

1815

時鳥馬をおどして通りけり

hototogisu uma wo odoshite tōri keri

the cuckoo hurls threats
at the horse
passing by

1816

時鳥なけなけ一茶是に有
hototogisu nake-nake issa kore ni ari

little cuckoo
sing! sing!
Issa is here

In the same year (the previous month, Fourth Month) Issa writes a similar haiku about a scrawny frog, ending with the same words: "Issa is here!"

1817

神ぎ祇や何れまことや時鳥
jingi gi ya izure makoto ya hototogisu

of all the gods
which ones are real?
cuckoo

1817

鳴まけなけふからえどの時鳥
naki makena kyō kara edo no hototogisu

from today on
let no one out-sing you!
Edo cuckoo

The cuckoo, like Issa, has come to the big city of Edo from the countryside. Issa encourages the newly arrived bird to out-sing everyone, perhaps a sly reference to his own ambitions as a haiku poet.

1817

這渡る橋の下より時鳥
hai-wataru hashi no shita yori hototogisu

crawling across a bridge
far below...
"Cuckoo!"

In his journal *Oraga haru* Issa copies this haiku with the headnote, "A Valley Wisteria Bridge." Daily Issa recipient Wendy King theorizes that the bridge may be made out of wisteria vines. "They feel very flimsy, sway above the roaring waters, and you really have to hold on to get across. They make them this way in Nepal, too." The editors of *Issa zenshū* share Wendy's theory (6.167).

1820

この闇に鼻つままれなほととぎす
kono yami ni hana tsumamare na hototogisu

in this darkness
don't get your nose picked!
cuckoo

Shinji Ogawa notes that there is an idiom, *hana tsumamare temo wakaranai hodo kurai* 鼻つままれても分からないほどくらい: "It's so dark you can't tell who's picking your nose." Issa plays with this expression in the present haiku and others.

1821

大降や業腹まぎれのほととぎす
ōburi ya gōhara magire no hototogisu

in heavy rain
seething with resentment
cuckoo

1821

本丸を尻目にかけてほととぎす
honmaru wo shirime ni kakete hototogisu

looking askance
at the great lord's fortress...
cuckoo

Issa refers here to an "inner citadel" (*honmaru* 本丸), where the lord of a castle lives; *KDJ* 1502. Is this a sly bit of political criticism? The cuckoo (like Issa?) seems to disdain pomp and power.

1824

時鳥江戸三界を夜もすがら

hototogisu edo sangai wo yo mo sugara

the cuckoo serenades
all of Edo
all... night... long!

year unknown

そつと鳴け隣は武士ぞ時鳥

sotto nake tonari wa bushi zo hototogisu

sing soft!
a samurai lives next door
cuckoo

1813

前の世のおれがいとこか閑古鳥

saki no yo no ore ga itoko ka kankodori

in a previous
life, my cousin?
mountain cuckoo

The mountain cuckoo (*kankodori* 閑古鳥) is a creature of the countryside, not the court (unlike the nightingale which is associated with the aristocracy). As a singer the bird is a sort

of poet. For these two reasons Issa may sense a deep
kinship.

1814

俳諧を囀るやうなかんこ鳥
haikai wo saezuru yōna kankodori

like warbling pure haiku
mountain
cuckoo

1815

かんこ鳥鳴や蟇どのの弔いに
kankodori naku ya hiki dono no tomurai ni

the mountain cuckoo sings
at Mr. Toad's
funeral

1822

鶯は籠で聞かよ閑古鳥
uguisu wa kago de kiku ka yo kankodori

does the caged
nightingale hear?
mountain cuckoo

1824

大酒の諫言らしや閑古鳥

ōzake no kangen-rashi ya kankodori

admonishing
my heavy drinking...
mountain cuckoo

1810

行々し下手盗人をはやすらん

gyōgyōshi heta nusubito wo hayasuran

cheered on
by a reed thrush
the incompetent thief

In the headnote to this haiku, Issa relates that a stranger attempted to steal a robe but was caught by the local citizens, tied to a bamboo pole, and run out of town—a spectacle that the poet describes as "entertaining"; *IZ* 2.572.

1812

よしきりのよしも一本角田川

yoshikiri no yoshi mo ippon sumida-gawa

just one reed
for the reed thrush...
Sumida River

よし切や一本竹のてつぺんに
yoshikiri ya ippon take no teppen ni

reed thrush
on a bamboo stalk's
tippy-top

1825

一村の鼾盛りや行々し
hito mura no ibiki-zakari ya gyōgyōshi

the village hits
a crescendo of snores...
reed thrush

1812

水鶏なく拍子に雲が急ぐぞよ
kuina naku hyōshi ni kumo ga isogu zo yo

to the rhythm
of a moorhen's cries...
a cloud speeds by

Or: "clouds speed by." R. H. Blyth imagines "clouds" in his translation; *A History of Haiku* (Tokyo: Hokuseido, 1964) 1.369. The bird (*kuina* 水鶏) is an Eastern water-rail. I follow

Blyth in translating it, "moorhen." Issa hears its calls and imagines a causal connection between them and the quickly passing cloud. We smile, at first, at the absurdity of a cloud moving to the rhythm of a moorhen's cries. But then, looking deeper, we ask: Isn't everything related? Issa thinks so.

1821
蛇も一皮むけて涼しいか
kuchinawa mo hito kawa mukete suzushii ka

with skin peeled off
snake
are you cool now?

1822
御仏の膝の上也蛇の衣
mi-hotoke no hiza no ue nari hebi no kinu

on Buddha's lap
a snake's forsaken
garment

1819

稲妻に天窓なでけり引蟇
inazuma ni atama nade keri hikigaeru

lightning flash—
the toad
rubs his head

1819

霧に乗る目付して居る蟇かな
kiri ni noru metsuki shite iru hiiki kana

looking like
"I can ride the fog!"...
a toad

1819

雲を吐く口つきしたり引蟇
kumo wo haku kuchi tsukishitari hikigaeru

his great mouth
burping clouds...
the toad

1819

罷出るは此薮の蟾にて候
makari izuru wa kono yabu no hiki nite sōrō

"Allow me to present myself—
I am the toad
of this thicket!"

Issa uses comically formal language in this haiku.

1792

馬の屁に目覚て見れば飛ほたる
uma no he ni mezamete mireba tobu hotaru

the horse's fart
wakes me to see...
fireflies flitting

1806

我家や町の蛍の逃所
waga ie ya machi no hotaru no nige-dokoro

my house
where the town's fireflies
hide out

1807

手の皺が歩み悪いか初蛍
te no shiwa ga arumi nikui ka hatsu-botaru

is my wrinkled hand
bad for walking?
first firefly

1809

蛍火や蛙もかうと口を明く
hotarubi ya kawazu mo kau to kuchi wo aku

sparkling fireflies—
even the frog's mouth
gapes

1811

子ありてや橋の乞食もよぶ蛍
ko arite ya hashi no kojiki mo yobu hotaru

they have kids too—
bridge beggars
calling fireflies

1811

さし柳蛍とぶ夜と成にけり

sashi yanagi hotaru tobu yo to nari ni keri

a night of fireflies
has arrived...
the willow I planted

1812

蛍よぶ口へとび入るほたる哉

hotaru yobu kuchi e tobi iru hotaru kana

a mouth calling fireflies—
one
flies in

1814

犬どもが蛍まぶれに寝たりけり

inu domo ga hotaru mabure ni netari keri

dogs sparkling
with fireflies
sound asleep

1815

牛の背を掃おろしたる蛍哉

ushi no se wo haki-orishitaru hotaru kana

sweeping them off
the cow's back...
fireflies

1815

蛍見の案内やするや庵の犬

hotaru mi no anai ya suru ya io no inu

guiding the way
to firefly-viewing...
the hut's dog

1816

我髪を薮と思ふかはふ蛍

waga kami wo yabu to omou ka hau hotaru

do you think
my hair's a thicket?
firefly

1816

わんぱくや縛れながらよぶ蛍
wanpaku ya shibarare nagara yobu hotaru

naughty child
though tethered calling
fireflies

1818

我袖に一息つくや負け蛍
waga sode ni hito iki tsuku ya make hotaru

on my sleeve
catching his breath...
worn-out firefly

1819

飛蛍其手はくはぬくはぬとや
tobu hotaru sono te wa kuwanu kuwanu to ya

flitting firefly—
uncaught by the hand
uncaught again!

1819

鼻紙に引つつんでもほたるかな

hana kami ni hittsutsunde mo hotaru kana

though wrapped in
tissue paper...
a firefly's light

1820

入相のかねにつき出す蛍哉

iriai no kane ni tsukidasu hotaru kana

evicted
from the sunset bell...
firefly

1821

かくれ家は蛍の休所哉

kakurega wa hotaru no yasumi-dokoro kana

secluded house—
a firefly
resort

1823

馬の屁に吹とばされし蛍哉
uma no he ni fuki-tobasareshi hotaru kana

blown away
by the horse's fart...
firefly

1824

木がくれの家真昼にとぶ蛍
kogakure no ie mappiru ni tobu hotaru

house in deep shade
at high noon...
fireflies

1825

湯上りの腕こそぐる蛍哉
yuagari no kaina kosoguru hotaru kana

after the bath
tickling my armpit...
firefly

1812

まゆひとつ仏のひざに作る也
mayu hitotsu hotoke no hiza ni tsukuru nari

one cocoon
in the stone Buddha's
lap

1820

どれ程に面白いのか火とり虫
dore hodo ni omoshiroi no ka hitorimushi

why is playing
with fire such fun...
tiger moth?

In this haiku Issa questions the moth's Japanese name, *hitorimushi* 火とり虫: "fire-taken bug." Tiger moths are drawn to fire, often to their deaths.

1823

大毛虫蟻の地獄におちにけり
ō kemushi ari no jigoku ni ochi ni keri

big caterpillar—
into the ants' hell
it has fallen

The "ants' hell" (*ari no jigoku* 蟻の地獄) is created by so-called antlions, whose predatory larvae dig pits to trap passing ants and other insects.

1813

ぼうふりや日にいく度のうきしづみ
bōfuri ya hi ni iku tabi no uki-shizumi

mosquito larvae—
in a day how many
ups and downs?

1806

目出度さは上総の蚊にも喰れけり
medetasa wa kazusa no ka ni mo kuware keri

a thing to celebrate!
the mosquitoes of Kazusa
feast on me too

Kazusa was an ancient province in the Kantō area. With tongue in cheek Issa celebrates the "joys" of travel.

1808

うつくしき花の中より薮蚊哉
utsukushiki hana no naka yori yabu ka kana

from deep inside
the pretty flower...
a mosquito

1811

夕空や蚊が鳴出してうつくしき
yūzora ya ka ga nakidashite utsukushiki

evening sky—
the whine of mosquitoes
pretty

1814

蚊柱の穴から見ゆる都哉
ka-bashira no ana kara miyuru miyako kana

through a hole
in the mosquito swarm...
Kyoto

The mosquitoes are swarming in a column (*ka-bashira* 蚊柱).

1816

それがしが宿は藪蚊の名所哉

soregashi ga yado wa yabu ka no meisho kana

my home—
for the mosquitoes
a famous site

1816

我宿は口で吹ても出る蚊哉

waga yado wa kuchi de fuite mo deru ka kana

my home
where I even exhale
mosquitoes

1820

草の葉に蚊のそら死をしたりけり

kusa no ha ni ka no sorajini wo shitari keri

on a blade of grass
the mosquito
plays dead

1824

隣から叩き出れて来る蚊哉

tonari kara tataki dasarete kuru ka kana

driven from next door
here they come...
mosquitoes

1808

蠅打に敲かれ玉ふ仏哉

hae uchi ni tatakare tamau hotoke kana

swatting a fly
but hitting
the Buddha

1814

蠅一つ打てはなむあみだ仏哉

hae hitotsu utte wa namu amida butsu kana

while swatting a fly
"All praise to Amida
Buddha!"

The *nembutsu* 念仏 prayer is "Namu Amida Butsu"—"All praise to Amida Buddha!" A Buddhist in the scene (perhaps Issa himself) is killing or attempting to kill a creature despite

259

Buddha's prohibition against taking life. Shinran, the founder of Issa's Pure Land sect, taught that following precepts is not the way to rebirth in Amida Buddha's Pure Land. So, on one level the fly-swatting Buddhist is simply acknowledging Shinran's doctrine: we are all sinful, and we can realize enlightenment only through the Other Power (*tariki* 他力) of Amida.

1815

留主にするぞ恋して遊べ庵の蝿
rusu ni suru zo koi shite asobe io no hae

while I'm away
enjoy your lovemaking
hut's flies

1819

笠の蝿もうけふからは江戸者ぞ
kasa no hae mō kyō kara wa edo mono zo

fly on my umbrella-hat
from today on
a citizen of Edo!

1819

人一人蝿も一つや大座敷
hito hitori hae mo hitotsu ya ōzashiki

one man, one fly
one large
sitting room

1820

長生の蝿よ蚤蚊よ貧乏村
nagaiki no hae yo nomi ka yo bimbo mura

living long
the flies, fleas, mosquitoes...
a poor village

1821

老の手や蝿を打さへ逃た跡
oi no te ya hae wo utsu sae nigeta ato

the old hand
swats a fly
already gone

261

1821

口明て蝿を追ふ也門の犬
kuchi akete hae wo ou nari kado no inu

gaping mouthed
and fly-hungry...
dog at the gate

1821

やれ打な蝿が手をすり足をする
yare utsuna hae ga te wo suri ashi wo suru

don't swat the fly!
rubbing hands
rubbing feet

In this famous haiku Issa sees the natural "hand-rubbing" behavior of the fly as hands praying, pleading to be spared. Adding a comic twist, he notes that the fly is praying even with its feet!

1822

打つて打つてと逃て笑ふ蝿の声
utte utte to nogarete warau hae no koe

swat! swat!
the escaping fly buzzes
with laughter

1823

人有れば蝿あり仏ありにけり
hito areba hae ari hotoke ari ni keri

where there's people
there's flies
and Buddhas

1823

むれる蝿皺手に何の味がある
mureru hae shiwade ni nanno aji ga aru

swarming flies
how do my wrinkled hands
taste?

1824

草庵にもどれば蝿ももどりけり
sōan ni modoreba hae mo modori keri

I go back in
my thatched hut...
the fly does the same

year unknown

豊年の声を上けり門の蝿

hōnen no koe wo age keri kado no hae

"It's a good year!"
they buzz...
flies at the gate

1825

僧正の頭の上や蝿つるむ

sōjō no atama no ue ya hae tsurumu

on the high priest's
head...
flies making love

1825

無常鐘蝿虫めらもよつくきけ

mujō-gane hae mushimera mo yokku kike

the bell of life passing—
O flies and worms
listen well!

This fun haiku parodies the battle cry of Chinzei Hachirō Tametomo, a twelfth century warrior and strongman.

1811

盃に蚤およぐぞよおよぐぞよ

sakazuki ni nomi oyogu zoyo oyogu zoyo

in a sake cup
a flea
swimming! swimming!

1812

蚤とぶや笑仏の御口へ

nomi tobu ya warai-botoke no ōkuchi e

a flea jumps
in the laughing Buddha's
mouth

1812

夕暮や大盃の月と蚤

yūgure ya ō sakazuki no tsuki to nomi

evening—
in a big sake cup
moon and a flea

1813

あばれ蚤我手にかかつて成仏せよ
abare nomi waga te ni kakatte jōbutsu seyo

pesky flea
caught in my hand
become a Buddha!

1813

有明や不二へ不二へと蚤のとぶ
ariake ya fuji e fuji e to nomi no tobu

dawn—
to Fuji! to Fuji!
fleas jumping off

1814

狭くともいざ飛習へ庵の蚤
semaku to mo iza tobinarae io no nomi

though it's cramped
practice your jumping!
hut's fleas

1817

蚤噛んだ口でなむあみだ仏哉

nomi kanda kuchi de namu amida butsu kana

the mouth that gnawed
a flea: "All praise
to Amida Buddha!"

1818

蚤の跡かぞへながらに添乳哉

nomi no ato kazoe nagara ni soeji kana

she counts flea bites
while her child
suckles

1819

とべよ蚤同じ事なら蓮の上

tobe yo nomi onaji koto nara hasu no ue

if you jump flea
jump
on the lotus

Since the lotus symbolizes a happy reincarnation and enlightenment, Issa's advice to his fleas is steeped in Buddhism. Issa used this poem as the starting verse of a *kasen* renku that he wrote with Kibō (a proprietor of a hot spring spa in Kawahara) in the same year.

1822
新畳蚤の飛ぶ音さはさはし
nii-datami nomi no tobu oto sawa-sawashi

a new tatami mat—
fleas jumping
bumpity bump!

1817
大川へ虱とばする美人哉
ōkawa e shirami tobasuru bijin kana

into the big river
tossing her lice...
pretty woman

1809
母恋し恋しと蝉も聞ゆらん
haha koishi koishi to semi mo kikoyuran

do you also miss
your mother?
cicada

This haiku, written on the twenty-first day of Fifth Month, 1809, has a headnote: "Visited my father's grave, stayed at Seigan Temple in Asano, paid a visit to Furuma Sekko, who has secluded himself in mourning for his mother." Issa lost his own mother at age three.

1812

むく犬や蝉鳴く方へ口を明く
muku inu ya semi naku kata e kuchi wo aku

the dog turns
in the cicada's direction...
mouth agape

1813

恋をせよ恋をせよせよ夏のせみ
koi wo seyo koi wo seyo seyo natsu no semi

go ahead, make love!
make love!
summer cicadas

1813

寺山や袂の下を蝉のとぶ

tera yama ya tamoto no shita wo semi no tobu

temple mountain—
buzzing into my sleeve
a cicada

1813

夏の蝉恋する隙も鳴にけり

natsu no semi koi suru hima mo naki ni keri

summer cicada—
even in his lovemaking break
singing!

1814

蝉鳴や物喰ふ馬の頬べたに

semi naku ya mono kuu uma no hobbeta ni

the cicada chirrs
on the grazing horse's
cheek

1815

小坊主や袂の中の蝉の声
ko bōzu ya tamoto no naka no semi no koe

little monk—
deep in his sleeve
singing, a cicada

1822

もろ蝉の鳴こぼれけり笠の上
moro-zemi no naki kobore keri kasa no ue

so many cicadas
singing and tumbling off...
umbrella-hat

1822

蜘の子はみなちりぢりの身すぎ哉
kumo no ko wa mina chirijiri no misugi kana

all the baby spiders
scatter
to make a living

1801

足元へいつ来りしよかたつぶり

ashi moto e itsu kitarishi yo katatsuburi

at my feet
when did you get here?
snail

1805

朝やけがよろこばしいかかたつぶり

asayake ga yorokobashii ka katatsuburi

does the red dawn
delight you
snail?

Issa alternates between calling snails *katatsuburi* and *katatsumuri.*

1810

朝雨やすでにとなりのかたつぶり

asa ame ya sude ni tonari no katatsuburi

morning rain—
look! next to me
a snail

1810

それなりに成仏とげよかたつぶり

sore nari ni jōbutsu toge yo katatsuburi

just as you are
become Buddha!
snail

1813

夕月や大肌ぬいでかたつぶり

yūzuki ya ōhada nuide katatsuburi

in evening moonlight
going bare-chested...
snail

1815

柴の門や錠のかはりのかたつぶり

shiba no to ya jō no kawari no katatsuburi

the brushwood door's
substitute lock...
a snail

1821

でで虫の其身其まま寝起哉

dedemushi no sono mi sono mama neoki kana

little snail, no different
asleep
awake

1824

戸を〆てづんづと寝たりかたつむり

to wo shimete zunzu to netari katatsumuri

closing the door
he drops off to sleep...
snail

Or: "she." If Issa wrote in English he certainly wouldn't refer to one of his "cousin" animals as an "it."

1823

野らの人の連に昼寝やかたつむり

nora no hito no tsure ni hirune ya katatsumuri

taking a siesta
with the farmer...
a snail

1812

夕顔の花で洟かむ娘かな

yūgao no hana de hana kamu musume kana

blowing her snot
on the moonflower...
a young girl

1812

夕顔の花で洟かむおばば哉

yūgao no hana de hana kamu o-baba kana

blowing her snot
on the moonflower...
granny

1810

生て居るばかりぞ我とけしの花

ikite iru bakari zo ware to keshi no hana

just being alive
I
and the poppy

1812

何をいふはりあひもなし芥子の花
nani wo iu hariai mo nashi keshi no hana

words
are a waste of time...
poppies

Whatever anyone can say is "not worth the trouble" (*hariai mo nashi* はりあひもなし). The flowers are so beautiful, they defy language to describe them, even the language of a poet.

1815

今日の志いふけしの花
konnichi no kokorozashi iu keshi no hana

speaking
this day's deepest thoughts...
poppies

1825

けし提てけん嘩の中を通いけり
keshi sagete kenka no naka wo tōri keri

carrying a poppy
he passes through
the quarrel

1792

散ぼたん昨日の雨をこぼす哉
chiru botan kinou no ame wo kobosu kana

the peony falls
spilling out yesterday's
rain

1809

猫の鈴ぼたんのあつちこつち哉
neko no rin botan no atchi kotchi kana

the cat's bell tinkling
in the peonies
here and there

1818

おのづから頭の下たるぼたん哉
onozukara zu no sagaritaru botan kana

by itself
the head is bowing...
peony!

Or: "my head."

1819

鶏の抱かれて見たるぼたん哉

niwatori no dakarete mitaru botan kana

sitting on her eggs
the hen admires
the peony

1825

つくづくとぼたんの上の蛙哉

tsuku-zuku to botan no ue no kawazu kana

a masterly climb
to the top of the peony...
frog

1806

蓮の花乞食のけぶりかかる也

hasu no hana kojiki no keburi kakaru nari

lotus blossoms—
the beggar's smoke
wafts over

1806

福蟇も這出給へ蓮の花
fuku-biki mo haiide tamae hasu no hana

Lucky the Toad
crawl out!
lotus blossom

1817

灯かげなき所が本んの蓮哉
hokage naki tokoro ga hon no harasu kana

in a place
where no light flickers
the perfect lotus

1822

さく蓮下水下水のおち所
saku harasu gesui gesui no ochi dokoro

blooming lotuses
where sewer water
pours

The lotuses are pure, despite the polluted water they grow in. In this way they are an emblem of Pure Land Buddhism: floating on the muddy waters of the world, unmuddied.

279

1822

人喰た虻が乗る也蓮の花
hito kūta abu ga noru nari hasu no hana

after feasting on people
the horsefly mounts
the lotus

Issa might be suggesting, playfully, a Buddhist lesson. After sinning (sucking people's blood), the ferocious little insect lands on the lotus blossom: a symbol of enlightenment. Thus the scene illustrates Shinran's teaching that even great sinners can be reborn in the Pure Land, if only they trust in Amida Buddha.

1812

御地蔵や花なでしこの真中に
o-jizō ya hana nadeshiko no man naka ni

holy Jizō
in the blooming pinks...
dead center

1794

垣津旗よりあの虹は起りけん
kakitsubata yori ano niji wa okoriken

irises—
where that rainbow
starts from

Issa imagines that the rainbow has arisen from blooming irises—the intense, showy colors of the flowers continuing in bold streaks upward, into the sky, forming the rainbow. It's interesting that "iris" derives from the Greek word for "rainbow." Issa could not have known this, but he intuits the same connection that exists in many Western languages. The rainbow is a flower in the sky; irises are rainbows on earth.

1814

さをしかの口とどかぬや杜若
saoshika no kuchi todokanu ya kakitsubata

the young buck's
mouth can't reach...
the iris

1818

小便のたらたら下や杜若
shōben no tara-tara dare ya kakitsubata

where piss dribbles,
dribbles down...
irises

1824

草家根やささぬ菖蒲は花がさく
kusa yane ya sasanu shōbu wa hana ga saku

thatched roof—
the irises piercing it
bloom

The night before the annual Boy's Festival (fifth day, Fifth Month), eaves of houses were thatched with grafts of blooming irises.

1803

我見ても久しき蟾や百合の花
ware mite mo hisashiki hiki ya yuri no hana

staring at me
on and on...
toad in the lilies

1810

けふからの念仏聞々ゆりの花

kyō kara no nebutsu kiki kiki yuri no hana

from today on
hear my "Praise Buddha!"
lilies

1812

さをしかの角にかけたりゆりの花

saoshika no tsuno ni kaketari yuri no hana

dangling from
the young buck's antler...
lilies

1812

夕闇やかのこ斑のゆりの花

yū yami ya kanoko madara no yuri no hana

evening gloom—
a fawn's spots
on the lily

1821

浮草にふはり蛙の遊山かな

ukikusa ni fuwari kawazu no yusan kana

so lightly
on the duckweed
the frog's picnic

1821

御鼠ちよろちよろ浮草渡り哉

on-nezumi choro-choro ukikusa watari kana

Sir Mouse
nimbly, nimbly crosses
the duckweed

1814

のさばるや黒い麦のほ里蜻蛉

nosabaru ya kuroi mugi no ho sato tombo

lording over
the black barley ears...
village dragonflies

1815

我上にやがて咲らん苔の花
waga ue ni yagate sakuran koke no hana

over me
soon enough you'll bloom
moss blossoms

1821

御地蔵の膝も眼鼻も苔の花
o-jizō no hiza mo mehana mo koke no hana

in holy Jizō's
lap, eyes, nose...
blooming moss

1819

少し見ぬうちに天晴若竹ぞ
sukoshi minu uchi ni appare waka take zo

while I was away
just for a while...
a splendid young bamboo!

1824

杖になる小竹もわか葉盛り哉

tsue ni naru ko take mo wakaba sakari keri

becoming a walking stick
little bamboo
at the peak of youth

1809

筍を見つめてござる仏哉

takenoko wo mitsumete gozaru hotoke kana

staring at the shoots
of new bamboo...
Buddha

1810

竹の子の兄よ弟よ老ぬ

takenoko no ani yo ototo yo toshiyorinu

bamboo shoots—
big brothers, little brothers
growing up

1820

竹の子や女のほじる犬のまね

takenoko ya onna no hojiru inu no mane

bamboo shoots—
a woman digs them up
like a dog

In this visually humorous haiku, Issa describes a woman digging up bamboo shoots as "imitating a dog" (*inu no mane* 犬のまね): her two hands working like a dog's front paws.

1809

瓜になれなれなれとや蜂さわぐ

uri ni nare nare nare to ya hachi sawagu

"Grow, grow, grow
melons!"
buzz the bees

1813

人来たら蛙になれよ冷し瓜

hito kitara kawazu to nare yo hiyashi uri

if someone comes
change into frogs!
cooling melons

1819

初瓜を引とらまへて寝た子哉

hatsu uri wo hittoramaete neta ko kana

first melon of the season

in her grasp...

sleeping child

Or: "his grasp."

year unknown

草の戸や一月ばかり冷し瓜

kusa no to ya hito tsuki bakari hiyashi uri

my hut—

the only cooling melon

is the moon

1821

若葉して猫と烏と喧嘩哉

wakaba shite neko to karasu to kenka kana

fresh new leaves—

the cat and the crow

quarrel

1821

上人が昼寝つかふや夏木立
shōnin ga hirune tsukau ya natsu kodachi

the holy man
grabs a siesta...
grove of summer trees

1825

人声に蛭の落る也夏木立
hitogoe ni hiru no ochiru nari natsu kodachi

hearing voices
the leech drops...
summer trees

1804

卯の花に蛙葬る法師哉
u no hana ni kawazu hōmuru hōshi kana

in deutzia blossoms
the priest buries
the frog

1804

卯の花や葬の真似する子ども達

u no hana ya sō no mane suru kodomotachi

deutzia blossoms—
the children play
funeral

1819

卯の花の吉日もちし後架哉

u no hana no kichi nichi mochishi kōka kana

with deutzia blossoms
on this lucky day...
outhouse

1821

卯の花に布子の膝の光哉

u no hana ni nunoko no hiza no hikari kana

deutzia blossoms
light up
my cotton-padded lap

Issa is wearing padded cotton clothing (*nunoko* 布子).

1821

卯の花や子供の作る土だんご
u no hana ya kodomo no tsukuru tsuchi dango

deutzia in bloom
the children make
mud-dumplings

.

1825

卯の花の垣根に犬の産屋哉
u no hana no kakine ni inu no ubuya kana

deutzia blossom hedge
the dog's
maternity room

1822

茨垣犬の上手に潜りけり
ibara kaki inu no jyōzu ni kuguri keri

thorn hedge—
the dog crawls through
like a pro

1823

下々国の茨も正覚とりにけり

gege koku no bara mo shōgaku tori ni keri

even wild roses
of a downtrodden land
reach enlightenment

7. AUTUMN

1804

立秋や旅止まくと思ふ間に
tatsu aki ya tabi yamemaku to omou ma ni

autumn begins—
I thought by now this journey
would've ended

1822

秋立といふばかりでも寒かな
aki tatsu to iu bakari demo samusa kana

"Autumn's begun"
just saying it
feels cold

1820

けさ秋としらぬ狗が仏哉
kesa aki to shiranu enoko ga hotoke kana

not knowing that
autumn's begun, puppy
Buddha!

1813

うそ寒や親といふ字を知つてから

uso samu ya oya to iu ji wo shitte kara

nippy weather—
the meaning of "parent"
sinks in

This haiku has the headnote, "Flowing through all the provinces for fifty years." Issa wrote it in Ninth Month, 1813. He was 51 (by Japanese reckoning) and had returned to his native village to settle down. The next year, he married, but already the idea of becoming a parent seems to have been on his mind.

1805

朝寒や蟇も眼を皿にして

asa-zamu ya hiki mo manako wo sara ni shite

morning cold—
the toad's eyes too
open wide

"Eyes like saucers" (*manako wo sara ni shite* 眼を皿にして) is a Japanese expression for eyes opened wide with surprise. The toad "also" seems astonished at the coldness of the morning, suggesting that Issa is just as surprised. The time for the frog's winter hibernation and the poet's winter seclusion is fast approaching.

1793

酒呑まぬ吾身一ッの夜寒哉
sake nomanu waga mi hitotsu no yozamu kana

out of sake
such is my life...
a cold night

1793

歯噛みする人に目覚て夜寒哉
hagami suru hito ni mezamete yozamu kana

his grinding teeth
wake me...
a cold night

1804

すりこ木もけしきに並ぶ夜寒哉
surikogi mo keshiki ni narabu yozamu kana

a pounding pestle
completes the scene...
a cold night

1820

鶏の小首を曲げる夜寒哉

niwatori no kokubi wo mageru yozamu kana

the chicken
tilts its head in wonder...
a cold night

1808

いななくや馬も夜寒は同じ事

inanaku ya uma mo yozamu wa onaji koto

for the neighing horse
the cold night
same as for me

1808

ことごとく仏の顔も夜寒哉

koto-gotoku hotoke no kao mo yozamu kana

one and all
faces of the Buddhas
cold tonight

1811

まじまじと梁上君の夜寒哉

maji-maji to ryōjōkun no yozamu kana

brazenly
the mouse sneaks in...
a cold night

Shinji Ogawa notes that *ryōjōkun* 梁上君 ("a gentleman on the beam") denotes "thief," but connotes, derivatively, "mouse." In this context, "mouse" seems to fit better.

1814

腹上で字を書習ふ夜寒哉

hara ue de ji wo kakinarau yozamu kana

practicing calligraphy
on my belly...
a cold night

1814

六十に二ッふみ込む夜寒哉

roku jū ni futatsu fumikomu yozamu kana

another year closer
to sixty...
the cold night

In 1814 Issa was 52 by Japanese reckoning. Literally, he says that two years have passed in his sixth decade.

1815

石橋を足で尋ねる夜寒哉

ishi-bashi wo ashi de tazuneru yozamu kana

feeling for the stone bridge
with my feet...
a cold night

1815

膝がしら山の夜寒に古びけり

hizagashira yama no yozamu ni furubi keri

my knees
this cold night in the mountains
feel older

1816

垣外へ屁を捨に出る夜寒哉

kaki soto e he wo sute ni deru yozamu kana

going outside the fence
to fart...
a cold night

1816

ぼつぼつと猫迄帰る夜寒哉
botsu-botsu to neko made kaeru yozamu kana

one by one
even the cats come home...
cold nights

Or: "a cold night."

1816

見上皺見下ル皺の夜寒哉
mi-age shiwa mi-sagaru shiwa no yozamu kana

looking up, wrinkles
looking down, wrinkles...
a cold night

1817

こほろぎの大声上る夜寒哉
kōrogi no ōkoe ageru yozamu kana

the cricket
cranks up the volume...
a cold night

The modern expression, "cranks up the volume," is my translation for Issa's middle phrase, "raises a big voice" (*ōkoe ageru* 大声上る).

1817
掌に藍染め込んで夜寒哉
tenohira ni ai some konde yozamu kana

dyeing the hands
indigo blue...
the cold night

1818
一人と書留らるる夜寒哉
ichi nin to kaki tomeraruru yozamu kana

"a man"
is registered at the inn...
a cold night

1818
盆の灰いろはを習ふ夜寒哉
bon no hai iroha wo narau yozamu kana

practicing writing
in the tray's ashes...
a cold night

A child is practising the A-B-C's of hiragana. The symbols *i-ro-ha* いろは begin a poem that includes all the hiragana symbols. In a rewrite of this haiku a year later (1819), Issa specifies that the person is a child.

1819

小便所ここと馬呼ぶ夜寒哉
shōbenjo koko to uma yobu yozamu kana

"Here's the outhouse!"
the horse calls...
a cold night

This haiku appears in one text with the headnote, "Being lost at the time." The editors of *Issa zenshū* speculate that Issa might have been staying at an unfamiliar house. Walking outside to relieve himself in the dark night, he went astray (6.174). The kind horse helped him find the outhouse.

1822

足で追ふ鼠が笑ふ夜寒哉
ashi de ou nezumi ga warau yozamu kana

the stomped-at mouse
squeaks with laughter...
a cold night

1822
窓際や虫も夜寒の小寄合
mado-giwa ya mushi mo yozamu no ko yoriai

at the window
insects too
a cold night huddle

year unknown
芦の穂を蟹がはさんで秋の夕
ashi no ho wo kani ga hasande aki no yū

crabs jamming themselves
in the cattails...
autumn night

1806
又人にかけ抜れけり秋の暮
mata hito ni kakenukare keri aki no kure

yet another traveler
overtakes me...
autumn dusk

1808

かたつむり何をかせぐぞ秋の暮
katasumuri nani wo kasegu zo aki no kure

O snail
how do you make your living?
autumn dusk

1811

なかなかに人と生れて秋の暮
naka-naka ni hito to umarete aki no kure

quite remarkable
being born human...
autumn dusk

This enigmatic poem is evidently one of Issa's favorites and most personally important, appearing first in a *haibun* and recopied in six other texts. The expression *naka-naka ni* なか なかに can mean either "remarkable" or "just so-so." Issa seems to be playing with both meanings; see *Issa and Being Human: Portraits of Early Modern Japan*, "Introduction."

1815

小猿めがきせる咥へて秋の暮

ko saru me ga kiseru kuwaete aki no kure

the little monkey
chews on a pipe...
autumn dusk

1816

馬の子も旅に立也秋の暮

uma no ko mo tabi ni tatsu nari aki no kure

the pony also
sets off on a journey...
autumn dusk

The pony has evidently been sold and now must leave its mother.

1816

又ことし死損じけり秋の暮

mata kotoshi shini-sonji keri aki no kure

another year
I didn't die...
autumn dusk

1820

それがしも宿なしに候秋の暮
soregashi mo yado nashi ni soro aki no kure

I too
without a home...
autumn dusk

1822

知つた名のらく書見へて秋の暮
shitta na no rakugaki miete aki no kure

I know this wall scribbler's
name...
autumn dusk

Or: "I know these wall scribblers' names." Issa recognizes a
name (or names) on a wall.

1823

小言いふ相手は壁ぞ秋の暮
kogoto yū aite wa kabe zo aki no kure

the only one to nag now
is the wall...
autumn dusk

1793

秋の夜や旅の男の針仕事
aki no yo ya tabi no otoko no harishigoto

autumn evening—
a traveling man busy
stitching

1804

秋の夜やよ所から来ても馬のなく
aki no yo ya yoso kara kite mo uma no naku

autumn evening—
from elsewhere another horse
neighs in reply

1811

秋の夜や窓の小穴が笛を吹
aki no yo ya mado no ko ana ga fue wo fuku

autumn evening—
wind in the window's little hole
plays flute

1803

ばか長き夜と申したる夜永哉
baka nagaki yo to mōshitaru yonaga kana

"It's a foolishly long
night!" I say
in the long night

1813

下駄からりからり夜永のやつら哉
geta karari karari yo naga no yatsura kana

wooden clogs
clomp! clomp!
a long, weary night

1812

十ばかり屁を棄てに出る夜永哉
jū bakari he wo sute ni deru yonaga kana

going out to fart
about ten times...
a long night

1813

蚤どもがさぞ夜永だろ淋しかろ

nomi domo ga sazo yonaga daro sabishi karo

for you fleas
the night must be long...
and lonely?

1813

うつくしやしようじの穴の天の川

utsukushi ya shōji no ana no ama no kawa

looking pretty
in a hole in the paper door...
Milky Way

1815

寝むしろやたばこ吹かける天の川

nemushiro ya tabako fukakeru ama no gawa

sleeping mat—
blowing pipe smoke
at the Milky Way

1820

冷水にすすり込だる天の川

hiya mizu ni susuri kondaru ama no gawa

in cold water
sipping the stars...
Milky Way

1826

盃に呑んで仕廻ふや天の川

sakazuki ni nonde shimau ya ama no gawa

in my sake cup
down the hatch!
the Milky Way

year unknown

霜おくやふとんの上の天の川

shimo oku ya futon no ue no ama no gawa

frost has formed
on the futon...
Milky Way above

1792

船頭よ小便無用浪の月

sendō yo shōben muyō nami no tsuki

hey boatman
no pissing on the moon
in the waves!

1803

投られし角力も交じる月よ哉

nagarareshi sumō mo majiru tsuki yo kana

the defeated wrestler, too
joins the crowd...
bright moon

1811

赤い月是は誰のじや子ども達

akai tsuki kore wa tare no ja kodomotachi

which of you owns
that red moon
children?

1811

婆々どのが酒呑に行く月よ哉

baba dono ga sake nomi ni yuku tsuki yo kana

granny walks along
drinking sake...
a moonlit night

1818

すつぽんと月と並ぶや角田川

suppon to tsuki to narabu ya sumida-gawa

the turtle and moon
merge...
Sumida River

1826

古壁やどの穴からも秋の月

furu kabe ya dono ana kara mo aki no tsuki

old wall—
from whichever hole
autumn moon

1798

名月のこころになれば夜の明る
meigetsu no kokoro ni nareba yo no akeru

harvest moon—
when my heart's had its fill
it's dawn

1805

雨降らぬ空も見へけり月一夜
ame furanu sora mo mie keri tsuki hito yo

in some sky
rain isn't falling...
harvest moon night

1808

いさらいに石あたたまる月よ哉
isarai ni ishi atatamaru tsuki yo kana

under my bottom
the stone warms up...
moonlit night

1808

名月の御覧の通り屑家也
meigetsu no goran no tōri kuzuya nari

lit by the harvest moon
no different...
trashy house

1810

名月をにぎにぎしたる赤子哉
meigetsu wo nigi-nigishitaru akago kana

trying and trying
to grasp the harvest moon—
toddler

1813

名月や家より出て家に入
meigetsu ya ie yori dete ie ni iru

harvest moon—
going out
going back in

1816

ふしぎ也生た家でけふの月
fushigi nari umareta ie de kyō no tsuki

amazing—
in the house I was born
seeing this moon

This haiku has the headnote, "Forty years of wandering." It was written in Eighth Month, 1816. Issa returned to his native village of Kashiwabara in 1813, after (nearly) forty years of exile.

1816

名月や山のかがしの袂から
meigetsu ya yama no kagashi no tamoto kara

harvest moon
on the mountain scarecrow's
sleeve

1819

庵のかぎ松にあづけて月見哉
io no kagi matsu ni azukete tsukimi kana

guard my hut's key
pine tree!
going moon-gazing

1819

酒尽て真の座に付月見哉

sake tsukite shin no za ni tsuku tsukimi kana

the sake gone
time to buckle down
and moon-gaze

1819

名月や五十七年旅の秋

meigetsu ya go jū nana nen tabi no aki

harvest moon—
fifty-seven years
of traveling autumns

1821

名月や出家士諸商人

meigetsu ya shukke samurai shoakindo

harvest moon-gazing
priests, samurai
merchants

Here Issa lists three of the four traditional social stations of
feudal Japan, the unnamed fourth class being farmers—
represented in the scene by the observing poet. All are

united in their moon-gazing.

1821

名月や茶碗に入れる酒の銭

meigetsu ya cha wan ni ireru sake no zeni

harvest moon—
digging in the teacup
for sake money

1821

名月や横に寝る人おがむ人

meigetsu ya yoko ni neru hito ogamu hito

harvest moon—
some are stretched out
some praying

Sakuo Nakamura, thinking about Issa's biography, pictures only two persons in the scene: Issa and his wife, Kiku, who would have been three months' pregnant at the time. Indeed, it is a sweet image, picturing the husband and wife: one lying down (Issa?) and one praying (Kiku?).

1822

名月に来て名月を鼾かな
meigetsu ni kite meigetsu wo ibiki kana

on harvest moon night
greeting the moon...
with snores

1823

小言いふ相手もあらばけふの月
kogoto yū aite mo araba kyō no tsuki

if only she were here
for nagging...
tonight's moon!

This haiku refers (fondly) to Issa's wife, Kiku, who died in 1823. It has the headnote, "My fault-finding old wife passed away this year."

1824

屁くらべや芋名月の草の庵
he kurabe ya imo meigetsu no kusa no io

a farting contest—
harvest moon night
in the hut

1804

売馬の親かへり見る秋の雨
uri uma no oya kaeri miru aki no ame

the sold pony
looks back at mother...
autumn rain

1809

かたつぶり何をかせぐぞ秋の雨
katatsuburi nani wo kasegu zo aki no ame

O snail
how do you make your living?
autumn rain

1809

薬呑む馬もありけり秋の雨
kusuri nomu uma mo ari keri aki no ame

the horse drinks
medicine too...
autumn rain

1813

放たる蚤の又来る秋の雨

hanasetaru nomi no mata kuru aki no ame

my evicted fleas
have returned...
autumn rain

1803

一人づつ皆去にけり秋の風

hitori-zutsu mina sari ni keri aki no kaze

one by one
everyone has left...
autumn wind

1804

秋の風乞食は我を見くらぶる

aki no kaze kojiki wa ware wo mikuraburu

autumn wind—
a beggar looking
sizes me up

1804

秋の風蝉もぶつぶつおしと鳴く
aki no kaze semi mo butsu-butsu oshi to naku

autumn wind—
the cicadas' grumbling
is louder

1805

秋風にあなた任の小蝶哉
aki kaze ni anata makase no ko chō kana

in autumn wind
trusting in the Buddha...
little butterfly

1806

うしろから秋風吹やもどり足
ushiro kara aki kaze fuku ya modori ashi

behind me
the autumn wind blows
me home

1806

どの星の下が我家ぞ秋の風

dono hoshi no shita ga waga ya zo aki no kaze

under which star
is my home?
autumn wind

1808

なけなしの歯を秋風の吹にけり

nakenashi no ha wo aki kaze no fuki ni keri

through what teeth
I have left
autumn's wind whistles

1810

秋風や腹の上なるきりぎりす

aki kaze ya hara no ue naru kirigirisu

autumn wind—
landing on my belly
a katydid

A katydid (*kirigirisu* きりぎりす) is a green or light brown insect, a cousin of crickets and grasshoppers. The males possess special organs on the wings with which they produce

321

shrill mating calls.

1825

秋の風一茶心に思ふやう
aki no kaze issa kokoro ni omou yō

autumn wind—
Issa's heart and mind
stirring

1813

秋風に歩行て逃る蛍哉
aki kaze ni aruite nigeru hotaru kana

in autumn wind
escaping on foot...
firefly

1814

膝節の古びも行か秋の風
hizabushi no furubi mo yuku ka aki no kaze

will these old knees
journey on?
autumn wind

1816

秋風の袂にすがる小てふ哉

aki kaze no tamoto ni sugaru ko chō kana

in the autumn wind
clutching my sleeve...
little butterfly

1817

秋の風宿なし烏吹かれけり

aki no kaze yado nashi karasu fukare keri

in autumn wind
a homeless crow
is blown

1819

秋風やむしりたがりし赤い花

aki kaze ya mushiritagarishi akai hana

autumn wind—
red flowers she wanted
to pick

This sad haiku has the headnote, "Sato, girl, 35th day, at the grave." It was the 35th day after the death of Issa's daughter, Sato. The red flowers that she would have liked to pick are blooming, but she is gone. Evidently, Issa has picked some of the flowers to leave at Sato's grave.

1825

淋しさに飯をくふ也秋の風
sabishisa ni meshi wo kū nari aki no kaze

eating my rice
in solitude...
autumn wind

1811

蚤の跡二人吹るる野分哉
nomi no ato futari fukaruru nowaki kana

blowing two people
after their fleas...
autumn gale

year unknown

いつぞやがいとまごひ哉墓の露
itsuzoya ga itomagoi kana haka no tsuyu

just the other day
we said goodbye...
dewy grave

1806

露の玉一ッ一ッに古郷あり

tsuyu no tama hitotsu hitotsu ni furusato ari

in beads of dew
one by one my home
village

1808

露置てうれしく見ゆる蛙哉

tsuyu oite ureshiku miyuru kawazu kana

happily watching
the dewdrops forming...
a frog

1810

白露にまぎれ込だる我家哉

shira tsuyu ni magire kondaru waga ya kana

in the silver dewdrops
vanishing...
my house

1810

露の世の露の中にてけんくわ哉

tsuyu no yo no tsuyu no naka nite kenka kana

amid dewdrops
of this dewdrop world
a quarrel

According to Jean Cholley, this haiku refers to Issa's inheritance dispute with his half-brother and stepmother; *En village de miséreux* 238.

1810

我門の宝もの也露の玉

waga kado no takara mono nari tsuyu no tama

a treasure at my gate
pearls
of dew

1811

白露にざぶとふみ込む烏哉

shira tsuyu ni zabu to fumi-komu karasu kana

into the silver dew
splashing struts
the crow

1813

露ちるやむさい此世に用なしと

tsuyu chiru ya musai kono yo ni yō nashi to

dewdrops scatter—
done with this crappy
world

1814

只頼め頼めと露のこぼれけり

tada tanome tanome to tsuyu no kobore keri

simply trust! trust!
dewdrops spilling
down

The haiku's message is that of Pure Land Buddhism. All that one can do in the face of death is to trust utterly in the liberating power of Amida Buddha to be reborn in the Pure Land.

year unknown

身の上の露ともしらでさはぎけり

mi no ue no tsuyu to mo shirade sawagi keri

unaware of life
passing like dewdrops...
they frolic

1817

我庵は露の玉さへいびつ也

waga io wa tsuyu no tama sae ibitsu nari

my hut—
where even beads of dew
are bent

1819

露の玉つまんで見たるわらべ哉

tsuyu no tama tsumande mitaru warabe kana

trying to pinch
a bead of dew...
a child

1819

露の世は露の世ながらさりながら

tsuyu no yo wa tsuyu no yo nagara sari nagara

this world
is a dewdrop world
yes... but...

According to Buddhist teaching, life is as fleeting as a dewdrop, and so one should not grow attached to the things of this world. However, Issa adds the phrase, "and yet..." His human heart clings to his daughter Sato, who died of smallpox.

1821

葉から葉に転びうつるや秋の露
ha kara ha ni korobi utsuru ya aki no tsuyu

from leaf to leaf
tumbling down...
autumn dew

1821

むだ草は露もむだ置したりけり
muda kusa wa tsuyu mo muda oku shitari keri

in vain grass
dewdrops forming
in vain

1819

稲妻につむりなでけり引蟇
inazuma ni tsumuri nade keri hikigaeru

in the lightning flash
rubbing his head...
toad

1820

稲妻に並ぶやどれも五十顔
inazuma ni narabu yadore mo go jū kao

in lightning's flash
faces in a row...
old men

I imagine that Issa is staying at an inn. When the lightning flashes, he sees, in a row, faces of old men (literally, men over age fifty).

1820

稲妻や狗ばかり無欲顔
inazuma ya enokoro bakari muyoku-gao

lightning flash—
only the puppy's face
is innocent

1822

稲妻やかくれかねたる人の皺
inazuma ya kakure kanetaru hito no shiwa

lightning flash—
no way to hide
the wrinkles

1805

朝霧の引からまりし柳哉

asa-giri no hikikaramarishi yanagi kana

the morning fog
tangled
in the willow

1807

山霧や声うつくしき馬糞かき

yama-giri ya koe utsukushiki ma-guso-kaki

mountain fog—
the beautiful voice
of the dung-hauler

1812

有明や浅間の霧が膳をはふ

ariake ya asama no kiri ga zen wo hau

dawn—
Mount Asama's fog on the dinner tray
crawls

Mount Asama, as mentioned earlier, was an active volcano in Issa's home province.

1814

大仏の鼻から出たりけさの霧
daibutsu no hana kara detari kesa no kiri

from the great bronze
Buddha's nostrils...
morning fog

1814

つりがねの中から霧の出たりけり
tsurigane no naka kara kiri no detari keri

pouring out
the hanging temple bell...
fog

1816

牛もうもうもうと霧から出たりけり
ushi mō mō mō to kiri kara detari keri

moo moo moo
from fog cows
emerge

1816

山霧の通り抜たり大座敷
yama-giri no tōri nuketari ōzashiki

mountain fog
just passing through...
big sitting room

1819

夕霧や馬の覚し橋の穴
yūgiri ya uma no oboeshi hashi no ana

evening fog—
the horse remembers
the bridge's hole

Or: "holes in the bridge."

1825

我宿は朝霧昼霧夜霧哉
waga yado wa asa-giri hiru-giri yo-giri kana

at my house
morning fog, noon fog
evening fog

1806

おく露は馬の涙か秋の山
oku tsuyu wa uma no namida ka aki no yama

is that dew
the horse's tears?
autumn mountain

1794

あぢきなや魂迎へ火を火とり虫
ajikina ya tama mukae hi wo hitorimushi

bad luck!
into the bonfire for the dead
a tiger moth

As mentioned in an earlier note, the moth's name in Japanese signifies a "a fire-taken bug." In this case, the moth loves the fire so much it perishes in the flame of a bonfire lit in honor of the spirits of the dead.

1810

迎へ火をおもしろがりし子供哉
mukaebi wo omoshirogarishi kodomo kana

delighted by bonfires
for the dead...
children

year unknown

末の子や御墓参りの箒持

sue no ko ya o-haka mairi no hōki mochi

the youngest child
on the grave visit
brings the broom

1823

古犬が先に立也はか参り

furu inu ga saki ni tatsu nari hakamairi

the old dog
leads the way...
visiting graves

1803

同じ年の顔の皺見ゆる灯籠哉

onaji toshi no kao no shiwa miyuru tōro kana

a wrinkled face
he's my age...
lanterns for the dead

1804

よ所事と思へ思へど灯ろ哉

yoso-goto to omoe omoedo tōro kana

someone else's affair
you think...
lanterns for the dead

Is this Issa's version of John Donne's admonition, "Ask not for whom the bell tolls;/ It tolls for thee"?

year unknown

かき立つて履見せる灯籠哉

kaki tatte hakimono miseru tōro kana

stoking it
to find my shoes...
lantern for the dead

1827

一つきへ二つきへつつ灯籠哉

hitotsu kie futatsu kie tsutsu tōro kana

one dies out
two die out...
lanterns for the dead

This is one of Issa's last haiku.

1815

嫁星の御顔をかくす榎哉
yome-boshi no o-kao wo kakusu enoki kana

veiling the face
of the Bride Star...
nettle tree

Tanabata is a festival that takes place on the seventh day of Seventh Month (early autumn in the old Japanese calendar). According to a romantic legend, two celestial lovers—the stars Altair and Vega—are separated by Heaven's River (the Milky Way). One night a year (Tanabata night), they cross the starry river to be together. In this haiku, the nettle tree hides the face of the (blushing?) "Bride Star" (*yome-boshi* 嫁星).

1822

鳴な虫別るる恋はほしにさへ
naku na mushi wakaruru koi wa hoshi ni sae

don't cry, insects—
lovers part
even among the stars

1824

大名の花火そしるや江戸の口
daimyō no hanabi soshiru ya edo no kuchi

griping about
the war lord's fireworks...
mouths of Edo

1821

手枕に花火のどうんどうん哉
temakura ni hanabi no dōn dōn kana

an arm for a pillow
fireworks boom!
ka-boom!

1821

どをんどんどんとしくじり花火哉
dōn don don to shikujiri hanabi kana

boom! boom! ka-boom!
so many duds...
fireworks

1825

一文の花火も玉や玉や哉
ichi mon no hanabi mo tamaya tamaya kana

even one-penny
fireworks...
ooo! ahh!

Shinji Ogawa notes that Tamaya is the name of a company that made fireworks in Issa's day. Praising the fireworks, the crowd shouts, "Tamaya!" Issa's humor lies in the fact that even cheap fireworks that cost only one *mon* are praised wildly.

1792

負角力其子の親も見て居るか
make-zumō sono ko no oya mo mite iru ka

defeated sumo wrestler—
is his father
watching too?

Or: "are his parents/ watching too?"

1814

角力とりやはるばる来る親の塚
sumōtori ya haru-baru kinuru oya no tsuka

the sumo wrestler
has come from afar...
parents' grave

Or: "father's grave" or "mother's grave." *Oya* 親 can signify one parent or two.

1821

乞食の角力にさへも贔屓かな
kojiki no sumō ni sae mo hiiki kana

even for the beggar—
a favorite
sumo wrestler

1823

勝角力虫も踏ずにもどりけり
kachi sumō mushi mo fumazu ni modori keri

sumo champion—
he won't even step
on a bug

A gentle giant.

1823

宮角力蛙も木から声上る

miya-zumō kawazu mo ki kara koe ageru

sumo match—
from trees the frogs, too
cheer

1824

風除に立てくれるや角力取

kazeyoke ni tatte kureru ya sumōtori

he makes a fine
wind-break...
sumo wrestler

1825

角力取が詫して逃す雀かな

sumōtori ga wabi shite nogasu suzume kana

the sumo wrestler
apologizing, releases
the sparrow

The wrestler is participating in a ritual of compassion in which a captive animal is released, a custom that originated in China.

1814

ぬつぽりと月見顔なるかがし哉
nuppori to tsukimi kao naru kagashi kana

that gentle
moon-gazing face...
a scarecrow

1805

とうとうと紅葉吹つけるかがし哉
tōtō to momiji fuki-tsukeru kagashi kana

a rush of red leaves
blown against him...
scarecrow

1808

かがし暮かがし暮けり人の顔
kagashi kure kagashi kure keri hito no kao

scarecrows at dusk
darkening...
human faces

1808

人に人かがしにかがし日の暮るる

hito ni hito kagashi ni kagashi hi no kururu

for people
and for scarecrows
the day ends

1816

天下泰平と立たるかがし哉

tenka taihei to tachitaru kagashi kana

standing in a world
of tranquility...
the scarecrow

1816

蜻蛉の寝所したるかがし哉

tombō no ne-dokoro shitaru kagashi kana

the dragonfly
settles to sleep...
on the scarecrow

1818

夕ぐれやかがしと我と只二人
yūgure ya kagashi to ware to tada futari

evening falls—
me and a scarecrow
just us two

1821

里犬のさつととがめるかがし哉
sato inu no satto togameru kagashi kana

the village dog
suddenly disapproves...
the scarecrow

1821

爺おやや仕舞かがしに礼を云
jiji oya ya shimau kagashi ni rei wo iu

packing away the scarecrow
grandpa pays
his respects

1821

我よりは若しかがしの影法師
ware yori wa wakashi kagashi no kagebōshi

looking younger than me
the scarecrow casts
his shadow

人はいさ直な案山子もなかりけり
hito wa isa suguna kagashi mo nakari keri

like people
an upright scarecrow
can't be found

1793

落し水魚も古郷へもどる哉
otoshi mizu uo mo kokyō e modoru kana

draining the rice field—
a fish also
heads home

In autumn when the rice is ready for harvest, farmers break the dikes that have kept the fields flooded. In this charming haiku Issa muses that a fish, too, is returning to its "native village" (*kokyō* 古郷)—an excellent example of his portrayal of animal behavior in human terms.

1809

こほろぎの声も添へけりおとし水
kōrogi no koe mo soe keri otoshi mizu

the cricket's song
is accompaniment...
the rice field drains

1804

えた町も夜はうつくしき砧哉
eta mura mo yo wa utsukushiki kinuta kana

in the outcastes' village too
a lovely night...
pounding cloth

In Japan and Korea, fulling-blocks were used to pound fabric and bedding. The fabric was laid over a flat stone, covered with paper, and pounded, making a distinctive sound. Since fulling-block is an arcane term that means nothing to most English readers, I follow Makoto Ueda in translating the action in the haiku, "pounding cloth"; *Matsuo Bashō* (Tokyo: Kodansha, 1982) 53.

1810

故郷や母の砧のよわり様
furusato ya haha no kinuta no yowari sama

home village—
mother's cloth-pounding
faintly heard

Issa wrote this nostalgic haiku forty-five years after his mother's death.

1813

隣とは合点しても小夜砧
tonari to wa gatten shite mo sayo-ginuta

my neighbor and I
have an understanding...
evening cloth-pounding

1819

梟が拍子とる也小夜ぎぬた
fukurō ga hyōshi toru nari sayo-ginuta

an owl hooting
to the beat...
evening cloth-pounding

1822

極楽に行かぬ果報やことし酒
gokuraku ni ikanu kahō ya kotoshi sake

this blessing
not allowed in Paradise...
new sake

Drinking alcoholic beverages is prohibited according to traditional Buddhist precepts. Issa doubts, therefore, that this "blessing" (*kahō* 果報) will be allowed in Amida Buddha's Western Paradise. As the words of a famous polka assert, "In heaven there is no beer; that's why we drink it here..." Though Issa was a Buddhist, he partook freely of the newly brewed sake, manifesting a healthy disdain for precept-following that is much in the tradition of the founder of the Jōdoshinshū sect to which he belonged, Shinran.

1825

小言いひいひ底たたく新酒哉
kogoto ii ii soko tataku shinshu kana

nagging, nagging—
the new sake
is drained

A scene of domestic less-than-perfection? Issa married then divorced his second wife the previous year.

1807

まどいして紅葉を祭る山の鹿

madoi shite momiji wo matsuru yama no shika

a little party
in the red leaves...
mountain deer

1813

鳴蝉に角をかしたる男鹿哉

naku semi ni tsuno wo kashitaru oshika kana

leasing his antler
to the cicada...
the young buck

1819

不精しか鳴放しにて寝たりけり

bushō shika naki-hanashi nite netari keri

the lazy buck
croons his mating call
lying down

1819

山寺や縁の上なるしかの声

yamadera ya en no ue naru shika no koe

mountain temple—
on the verandah
a deer cries

1822

さをしかの角に結びし手紙哉

saoshika no tsuno ni musubishi tegami kana

tied to the young
buck's antler...
a letter

1822

鹿鳴や川をへだてて忍ぶ恋

shika naku ya kawa wo hedatete shinobu koi

they cry to each other
across a river
deer in love

This image of lovers separated by a river alludes to the Tanabata legend, in which the river separating the celestial lovers is "Heaven's River," the Milky Way.

1822

ほたへるや犬なき里の鹿の声

hotaeru ya inu naki sato no shika no koe

barking—
in a village without dogs
cries of deer

1819

啄木の目利して見る庵哉

kitsutsuki no mekiki shite miru iori kana

the woodpecker
sizes it up...
my hut

1811

門の雁いくら鳴ても米はなき

kado no kari ikura naite mo kome wa naki

geese at my gate
cry all you like...
no rice

1811

雁の首長くして見る門口哉
kari no kubi nagaku shite miru kado-guchi kana

stretching her neck
the goose peeks in
my gate

1811

田の雁や里の人数はけふもへる
ta no kari ya sato no ninzu wa kyō moeru

rice field geese—
the village's population
surges

1812

跡の雁やれやれ足がいたむやら
ato no kari yare-yare ashi ga itamu yara

the rear goose—
well, well
a sore foot

1812

けふからは日本の雁ぞ楽に寝よ

kyō kara wa nihon no kari zo raku ni ne yo

from today on
you are Japanese geese...
rest easy

1813

鳴な雁どつこも同じうき世ぞや

naku na kari dokko mo onaji ukiyo zoya

don't cry, geese—
everywhere, the same
floating world

Geese migrating south for the winter honk noisily. Issa, as he likes to do, addresses them directly, consoling them that, no matter where they travel, they will always be in the same world of sorrow. Is the poem an invitation for the geese to stop their restless journey and settle down? Of course, they won't settle, and as they fly away Issa's thoughts and heart go with them.

1815

我が門に来て痩雁と成にけり
waga kado ni kite yase kari to nari ni keri

begging at my gate
the geese lose
weight

1819

得手物の片足立や小田の雁
ete mono no kata ashi-dachi ya oda no kari

a talented one
posed on one foot...
rice field goose

1820

開帳の跡をかりてや雁の鳴
kaichō no ato wo karite ya kari no naku

in the wake
of the Buddhist procession...
honking geese

1813

雁とぶや門の家鴨も貰ひ鳴

kari tobu ya kado no ahiru mo morai naki

geese flying south—
the ducks at the gate
cheer them on

1825

門の雁我帰つてもねめつける

kado no kari ware kaette mo nemetsukeru

geese at my gate—
when I return
how they glare!

1809

渡り鳥日本の我を見しらぬか

watari-dori nihon no ware wo mishiranu ka

migrating birds
haven't you seen me before
in Japan?

1822

雀らも真似してとぶや渡り鳥
suzumera mo mane shite tobu ya watari-dori

the copycat sparrows
fly along...
migrating birds

1820

蛇の穴阿房鼠が入にけり
hebi no ana ahō nezumi ga iri ni keri

into the snake's hole
O foolish
mouse

Snakes entering their holes is an autumn season word. Here, Issa switches things around by having a mouse entering the hole instead.

1821

穴に入蛇も三人ぐらし哉
ana ni iru hebi mo sannin-gurashi kana

another snake
into the hole...
three roommates

1821

それ也になる仏いたせ穴の蛇
sore nari ni narubutsu itase ana no hebi

just as you are
become Buddha!
snake in your hole

1821

古蛇やはや西方の穴に入
furu hebi ya haya saihō no ana ni iru

the old snake
toward the Western Paradise
enters his hole

1821

来年は蝶にでもなれ穴の蛇
rainen wa chō ni demo nare ana no hebi

next year
become a butterfly!
snake in your hole

1808

夜涼みのかぎりを鳴やかごの虫
yo suzumi no kagiri wo naku ya kago no mushi

singing all
the cool night long...
caged insect

1814

青い虫茶色な虫の鳴にけり
aoi mushi chairona mushi no naki ni keri

green insect
and brown insect...
a duet

1818

籠の虫妻恋しとも鳴ならん
kago no mushi tsuma koishi tomo nakunaran

the caged insect
sings a love song
to his wife

In Japanese, Issa is less definite than in my English translation: the caged insect "is probably singing" (*nakunaran* 鳴ならん) to his wife.

1820

世の中や鳴虫にさへ上づ下手
yo no naka ya naku mushi ni sae jyōzu heta

in this world
among insects too...
good singers, bad singers

1821

寒いとて虫が鳴事始るぞ
samui tote mushi ga nakigoto hajimaru zo

"It's cold!"
the insects' complaining
has begun

year unknown

鳴ながら虫の流るる浮木かな
naki nagara mushi no nagaruru ukigi kana

still singing
the insect drifts away...
floating branch

1819

虫の屁を指して笑ひ仏哉
mushi no he wo yubisashite warai-botoke kana

pointing
at the fart bug...
laughing Buddha

The "fart bug" (bombardier beetle) is a stink bug that protects itself with well-aimed, explosive farts.

1820

御仏の鼻の先にて屁ひり虫
mi-hotoke no hana no saki nite hehirimushi

on the tip
of Buddha's nose...
a fart bug

1804

あのやうに我も老しか秋のてふ
ano yō ni ware mo oishi ka aki no chō

will I grow old
like you?
autumn butterfly

Issa wrote this haiku at age 42. Butterflies are a spring season word in haiku, so an autumn butterfly isn't long for this world.

1813

秋のてふかがしの袖にすがりけり
aki no chō kagashi no sode ni sugari keri

autumn butterfly
on the scarecrow's sleeve
clinging

year unknown

夕日影町いつぱいのとんぼ哉
yū hikage machi ippai no tombo kana

sunset—
the town is buzzing
with dragonflies

1813

蜻蛉の尻でなぶるや角田川
tombō no shiri de naburu ya sumida-gawa

the dragonfly
dips his butt...
Sumida River

361

1815

大犬の天窓張たる蜻蛉哉
ōinu no atama haritaru tombo kana

resting
on the big dog's head
dragonfly

1816

蜻蛉の夜かせぎしたり門の月
tombō no yo kasegi shitari kado no tsuki

the dragonfly goes about
his night work...
moon at the gate

1817

御祭の赤い出立の蜻蛉哉
o-matsuri no akai dedachi no tombo kana

departing for the festival
all in red
dragonfly

1820

遠山が目玉にうつるとんぼ哉

tōyama ga medama ni utsuru tombo kana

the distant mountain
reflected in his eyes...
dragonfly

1821

蜻蛉が鹿のあたまに昼寝哉

tombō ga shika no atama ni hirune kana

the dragonfly
on the deer's head...
a siesta

1825

蜻蛉やはつたとにらむふじの山

tombō ya hatta to niramu fuji no yama

the dragonfly's
steady glare...
Mount Fuji

1825

こほろぎが顔こそぐつて通りけり

kōrogi ga kao kosogutte tōri keri

a cricket
tickling my face
passes by

1812

こほろぎや子鹿の角のてんぺんに

kōrogi ya koshika no tsuno no tenpen ni

cricket—
on the young buck's antler's
tip

1820

こほろぎのうけ泊て鳴竈かな

kōrogi no uketomete naku kamado kana

deep inside
a cricket is singing...
oven

1793

鞍壷に三ッ四ッ六ッいなご哉

kuratsubo ni mittsu yotsu mutsu inago kana

on the saddle
three, four, six...
locusts

1810

枯々の野辺に恋するいなご哉

kare-gare no nobe ni koi suru inago kana

making love
in the withered fields...
locusts

year unknown

我死なば墓守となれきりぎりす

ware shinaba haka mori to nare kirigirisu

when I die
guard my grave
katydid!

Though this is an early haiku written in the 1790s, it's a possible candidate for Issa's death verse. He asks the little insect to guard his grave and, we presume, to continue his poetic legacy by "singing" over it.

1810

庵の夜や棚捜しするきりぎりす

io no yo ya tana sagashi suru kirigirisu

night in the hut—
a katydid forages
for food

1812

猫の飯打くらひけりきりぎりす

neko no meshi uchikurai keri kirigirisu

gorging himself
on the cat's food...
katydid

1813

今掃し箒の中のきりぎりす

ima hakishi hōki no naka no kirigirisu

inside the broom
I'm sweeping with...
a katydid

1813

妻やなきしはがれ声のきりぎりす

tsuma ya naki shiwagare koe no kirigirisu

still no wife
his voice grows hoarse...
katydid

Issa married his first wife, Kiku, the following year.

1814

野ばくちや銭の中なるきりぎりす

no bakuchi ya zeni no naka naru kirigirisu

gambling in the field—
in the pot
a katydid!

1816

白露の玉ふみかくなきりぎりす

shira tsuyu no tama fumikaku na kirigirisu

don't crush
the dewdrop pearls!
katydid

1816

寝返りをするぞそこのけきりぎりす

negaeri wo suru zo soko noke kirigirisu

turning over in bed—
move aside!
katydid

1816

山犬の穴の中よりきりぎりす

yama inu no ana no naka yori kirigirisu

crawling out
the wild dog's hole...
a katydid

1819

きりぎりすかがしの腹で鳴にけり

kirigirisu kagashi no hara de naki ni keri

a katydid
in the scarecrow's gut
singing

1820

きりぎりす身を売れても鳴にけり
kirigirisu mi wo urarete mo naki ni keri

the katydid—
even while they sell him
singing

1820

ほつけよむ天窓の上やきりぎりす
hokke yomu atama no ue ya kirigirisu

atop the scripture
reader's head...
a katydid

1815

蟷螂が片手かけたりつり鐘に
tōrō ga katate kaketari tsurigane ni

the praying mantis
hangs by one hand...
temple bell

369

1808

狼の毛ずれの草の咲にけり

ōkami no kezure no kusa no saki ni keri

in grass where the wolf
shed his fur...
wildflowers

1807

里犬の尿をかけけり菊の花

sato inu no bari wo kake keri kiku no hana

watered by
the village dog...
chrysanthemum

1814

片隅や去年勝たる菊の花

kata sumi ya saru nen kachitaru kiku no hana

off in a corner
last year's champion
chrysanthemum

1817

大名を味方にもつやきくの花
daimyō wo mikata ni motsu ya kiku no hana

the war lord
has pull...
chrysanthemum contest

Issa concludes with the phrase "chrysanthemum blossom(s)"
(*kiku no hana* きくの花), which I have translated, "chrysan-
themum contest" in an attempt to inject a shade of meaning
that exists in the diary context though not in the haiku
itself. This haiku is the second of three in Issa's journal on the
topic of losing a chrysanthemum contest to a daimyō. The
three poems, written at the beginning of Ninth Month, 1817,
evidently reflect a real-life injustice; *IZ* 3.492.

1817

人間がなくば曲らじ菊の花
ningen ga nakuba magaraji kiku no hana

if it weren't for people
they'd not grow crooked...
chrysanthemums

1819

藪菊のこつそり独盛りけり
yabu-giku no kossori hitori sakari keri

the thicket's chrysanthemum
blooms
in secret

1819

我やうにどつさり寝たよ菊の花
waga yō ni dossari neta yo kiku no hana

like me
getting plenty of sleep...
chrysanthemum

1822

隠家の糧にもなるやきくの花
kakurega no kate ni mo naru ya kiku no hana

it too becomes food
in the secluded house...
chrysanthemum

1822

酒呑まぬ者入べからず菊の門
sake nomanu mono irubekarazu kiku no kado

nondrinkers
stay out!
gate to the chrysanthemums

1823

大菊のてつぺんに寝る毛虫哉
ōgiku no teppen ni neru kemushi kana

atop the big chrysanthemum
asleep...
caterpillar

1805

朝顔に片肌入れし羅漢哉
asagao ni katahada ireshi rakan kana

into morning-glories
with one shoulder bare...
holy man

1805

あさがほに咲なくさるる小家哉
asagao ni saki nakusaruru ko ie kana

lost
in the morning-glories
little house

1805

朝顔に雫拵へて居りけり
asagao ni shizuku koshiraete suwari keri

droplets forming
on the morning-glories...
sitting still

1811

我庵は朝顔の花の長者哉
waga io wa asagao no hana no chōja kana

my hut
with its morning-glories
a palace

1812

朝顔の花で葺たる庵哉

asagao no hana de fukitaru iori kana

thatched with
morning-glories
my little hut

1815

朝顔の花に顔出す鼠かな

asagao no hana ni kao dasu nezumi kana

in the morning-glories
peeking out...
a mouse

1824

朝顔に涼しくくふやひとり飯

asagao ni suzushiku kuu ya hitori meshi

in cool morning-glories
eating my rice
alone

1811

のら猫も宿と定る萩の花

nora neko mo yado to sadamuru hagi no hana

the stray cat also
picks this inn...
bush clover blooming

1806

おく露は馬の涙か稲の花

oku tsuyu wa uma no namida ka ine no hana

is that dew
the horse's tears?
rice blossoms

1809

我門は稲四五本の夕哉

waga kado wa ine shi go hon no yūbe kana

four or five rice stalks
at my gate...
evening falls

1819

蜻蛉もおがむ手つきや稲の花
tombō mo ogamu te tsuki ya ine no hana

the dragonfly too
folds hands in prayer...
rice blossoms

1820

稲の花大の男のかくれけり
ine no hana ō no otoko no kakure keri

rice blossoms—
a large man
lost in them

1822

半分は汗の玉かよ稲の露
hambun wa ase no tama ka yo ine no tsuyu

is half of it
human sweat?
rice field dew

Now that the rice is ready for harvest, Issa is reminded of all the toil that went into it.

1812

誰ぞ来よ来よとてさわぐすすき哉
tare zo ko yo ko yo tote sawagu susuki kana

come one! come all!
the rustling
plume grass

Shinji Ogawa notes, "The movements of plume grass in the wind resemble the Japanese beckoning gesture (palm side-down)."

1820

子どもらが狐のまねもすすき哉
kodomora ga kitsune no mane mo susuki kana

the children
pretend to be foxes...
plume grass

1820

幽霊と人は見るらんすすき原
yūrei to hito wa miruran susuki-bara

where people
see ghosts...
field of plume grass

1821

猫の子のまま事をするすすき哉
neko no ko no mamagoto wo suru susuki kana

the kittens
play house
in the plume grass

1805

山畠は鼠の穴も紅葉哉
yama hata wa nezumi no ana mo momiji kana

mountain field—
the mouse's hole too
under red leaves

1809

鶯がさくさく歩く紅葉哉
uguisu ga saku-saku aruku momiji kana

the nightingale struts
crunch crunch...
red leaves

1811

紅葉たく人をじろじろ仏哉
momiji taku hito wo jiro-jiro hotoke kana

staring at the man
burning leaves...
stone Buddha

1822

折々に小滝をなぶる紅葉哉
ori-ori ni ko taki wo naburu momiji kana

taking turns
down the little waterfall...
red leaves

1814

寝た犬にふはとかぶさる一葉哉
neta inu ni fuwa to kabusaru hito ha kana

on the sleeping dog
gently, a hat...
a leaf

The phrase, "one leaf" (*hito ha* 一葉), specifically denotes a paulownia leaf in the shorthand of haiku.

1818

そつくりと蛙の乗し一葉哉

sokkuri to kawazu no norishi hito ha kana

down it comes
with a frog rider...
the leaf

1819

頰べたにあてなどするや赤い柿

hōbeta ni ate nado suru ya akai kaki

holding it
against her cheek...
the red persimmon

This haiku has the headnote, "My daughter Sato dreaming." In a similar haiku written that year, the girl holds a muskmelon against her cheek while she sleeps.

year unknown

てふてふのいまだにあかぬ木槿哉

chōchō no imada ni akanu mukuge kana

butterflies never
tire of them...
roses of Sharon

1805

酒冷すちよろちよろ川の槿哉

sake hiyasu choro-choro kawa no mukuge kana

a babbling brook
chills the sake...
roses of Sharon

1822

洪水の泥の一花木槿かな

kōzui no doro ni hito hana mukuge kana

in the mud
after the flood, one rose
of Sharon

This haiku refers to a flood in Issa's home province of Shinano in Seventh Month, 1822. It is one of three in a row on this subject in his journal, *Shichiban nikki* 七番日記 ("Seventh Diary"). The single bloom on the shrub is a pitiful sight in the mud after the flood, but it is also an image of hope.

1804

闇の夜に段々なるぞ種瓢
yami no yo ni dan-dan naru zo tane fukube

in the gloom of night
bit by bit it grows...
the gourd

Or, more literally, "the seed gourd" (*tane fukube* 種瓢). Though the kanji for "gourd" is today commonly read as *hisago*, Issa read it as *fukube*.

1812

老たりな瓢と我が影法師
oitari na fukube to ware ga kagebōshi

the aging gourd
and I
cast our shadows

1806

栗おちて一つ一つに夜の更る
kuri ochite hitotsu hitotsu ni yo no fukeru

chestnuts dropping
one by one...
the night deepens

1806

芝栗や馬のばりしてうつくしき
shibaguri ya uma no bari shite utsukushiki

little chestnuts
pissed on by the horse...
shiny new

1813

大栗や漸とれば虫の穴
ōguri ya yōyaku toreba mushi no ana

after great effort
picking the big chestnut...
a wormhole

1816

茹栗と一所に終るはなし哉
yude-guri to isshō ni owaru hanashi kana

with the boiled chestnuts
finished, so is
the conversation

1821

おち栗や仏も笠をめして立
ochi-guri ya hotoke mo kasa wo meshite tatsu

chestnuts dropping—
even the stone Buddha
with umbrella-hat!

1821

ぱしぱちは栗としらるる雨夜哉
pachi-pachi wa kuri to shiraruru amayo kana

the pitter-patter
of falling chestnuts...
a rainy night

1827

馬の子の踏潰しけり野良の栗
uma no ko no fumi-tsubushi keri nora no kuri

the pony stepping
and crunching...
chestnuts in the field

1827

せま庭の横打栗やどろぼ猫
sema niwa no yoko utsu kuri ya dorobo neko

knocking chestnuts
out of the little garden...
thief cat!

1813

うつくしやあら美しや毒きのこ
utsukushi ya ara utsukushi ya doku kinoko

it's so pretty!
so pretty!
the poison mushroom

1819

五六人只一ッ也きの子がり
go roku nin tada hitotsu nari kinoko-gari

for five or six people
only one...
mushroom hunting

1813

行秋を尾花もさらばさらば哉
yuku aki wo obana mo saraba saraba kana

even plume grass
waves farewell, farewell...
to autumn

8. WINTER

1810

十月の中の十日の霰哉
jūgatsu no naka no tōka no arare kana

Tenth Month
on the tenth day...
hail

The first day of Tenth Month was the beginning of winter in the old Japanese calendar.

1824

薄壁や鼠穴より寒が入
usu kabe ya nezumi ana yori kan ga iru

thin wall—
from the mouse's hole
the cold

Two years earlier (1822) Issa wrote the same first two lines but had a wren as the surprise coming in from the hole.

year unknown

我好て我する旅の寒さ哉

ware sukite ware suru tabi no samusa kana

though I'm loving
these travels of mine...
it's cold!

This is an early haiku written in the 1790s.

1803

掌に酒飯けぶる寒さ哉

tenohira ni sakameshi keburu samusa kana

palms
in the cooking smoke
winter cold

1813

草庵は夢に見てさへ寒さ哉

sōan wa yume ni mite sae samusa kana

in my thatched hut
even dreaming
the cold

1816

古盆の灰で手習ふ寒さ哉
furu bon no hai de tenarau samusa kana

drawing words
in an old tray's ashes...
winter cold

1819

狼は糞ばかりでも寒さかな
ōkami wa kuso bakari demo samusa kana

merely the sight
of wolf shit...
how cold it is!

1819

古札の藪にひらひら寒さ哉
furu fuda no yabu ni hira-hira samusa kana

the old banner
flaps in a thicket
in the cold

1821

極楽が近くなる身の寒さ哉
gokuraku ga chikaku naru mi no samusa kana

drawing nearer
to the Pure Land...
life's cold winter

1815

うら口や曲げ小便もはつ氷
uraguchi ya mage shōben mo hatsu kōri

back door—
pissing scribbles
in the first ice

1815

福鼠渡り返せやはつ氷
fuku nezumi watari kaese ya hatsu kōri

the lucky mouse
crossing, come back!
first ice

1817

我家の一つ手拭氷りけり

waga ie no hitotsu tenugui kōri keri

my house's
only hand towel
frozen stiff

1820

すいすいと渡れば渡る氷哉

suisui to watareba wataru kōri kana

if you cross it
cross lightly!
ice

In one of his journals, Issa prefaces this haiku with the note, "Lake Suwa." The surface of Lake Suwa in his home province of Shinano freezes in the winter, but underwater hot springs keep the lower waters warm.

1824

猫の目や氷の下に狂ふ魚

neko no me ya kōri no shita ni kuruu uo

under the ice
the cat's eyes follow...
crazy fish

1824

本馬のしやんしやん渡る氷哉

hon uma no shan-shan wataru kōri kana

the packhorse crosses
tat-a-tat...
the ice

1814

御仏の御鼻の先へつらら哉

mi-hotoke no o-hana no saki e tsurara kana

on honorable Buddha's
honorable nose
an icicle

1816

僧正の天窓で折し氷柱哉

sōjō no atama de orishi tsurara kana

using his head
the high priest breaking
icicles

1817

野仏の御鼻の先の氷柱哉

no-botoke no o-hana no saki no tsurara kana

from the tip
of the field Buddha's nose...
an icicle

1822

山寺は鋸引の氷柱かな

yamadera wa nokogiribiki no tsurara kana

mountain temple—
with a pull-saw cutting
icicles

1792

外堀の割るる音あり冬の月

sotobori no waruru oto ari fuyu no tsuki

the ice of the moat
cracking...
winter moon

1816

石切のかちかち山や冬の月

ishikiri no kachi-kachi yama ya fuyu no tsuki

the stonecutter
chop-chops the mountain...
winter moon

1811

寒月や喰つきさうな鬼瓦

kangetsu ya kui tsuki sōna onigawara

like he's biting
the cold moon...
gargoyle

1806

かたつぶり我と来て住め初時雨

katatsuburi ware to kite sume hatsu shigure

come in snail
and live with me...
first winter rain

1810

初時雨俳諧流布の世也けり
hatsu shigure haikai rufu no yo nari keri

first winter rain—
the world drowns
in haiku

1812

山寺の茶に焚かれけりはつ時雨
yamadera no cha ni takare keri hatsu shigure

tea is steaming
at the mountain temple…
first winter rain

1812

初時雨走り入けり山の家
hatsu shigure hashiri iri keri yama no ie

first winter rain—
a mad dash
to the mountain house

1823

素湯を煮る伝授する也はつ時雨

sayu wo nieru denju suru nari hatsu shigure

she learns how to
boil water...
first winter rain

In the very next haiku in Issa's journal (Tenth Month, 1823), someone is taught to cook tofu. In both cases, I picture a little girl being taught by her mother or grandmother.

1803

北時雨火をたく顔のきなくさき

kita shigure hi wo taku kao no kinakusaki

cold northern rain—
the fire-starter's face
smells burnt

1803

しぐるるや牛に引かれて善光寺

shigururu ya ushi ni hikarete zenkōji

winter rain—
led by a cow
to Zenkō Temple

1810

しぐるるや苦い御顔の仏達
shigururu ya nigai o-kao no hotoke-tachi

in winter rain
how they scowl...
the Buddhas

Issa could be talking about statues of Buddha or people making grouchy faces.

1813

人のためしぐれておはす仏哉
hito no tame shigurete owasu hotoke kana

for our sake enduring
the winter rain...
stone Buddha

1810

又犬にけつまづきけり小夜時雨
mata inu ni ketsumazuki keri sayo shigure

tripping over the dog
again...
night of winter rain

1812

しぐるるや闇の図星を雁のなく

shigururu ya yami no zuboshi wo kari no naku

in winter rain
toward the heart of darkness...
honking geese

1814

おそろしや狼よりももる時雨

osoroshi ya ōkami yori mo moru shigure

a scary sight
worse than a wolf!
winter rain leaking in

1814

座頭の坊中につつんで時雨けり

zato no bō naka ni tsutsunde shigure keri

tucking in
the blind priest...
winter rain

1814

蛤のつひのけぶりや夕時雨

hamaguri no tsui no keburi ya yūshigure

the clams' cremation smoke
rises...
evening's winter rain

The rising steam from the pot, Issa imagines with deep and genuine sympathy, is the clams' cremation smoke.

1814

一ッ家や馬も旅人もしぐれ込

hitotsu ya ya uma mo tabibito mo shigure komu

huddled in one house
travelers, horses...
winter rain

year unknown

山鳩が泣事をいふしぐれ哉

yama-bato ga nakigoto wo iu shigure kana

the mountain pigeon
grumbles...
winter rain

1819

重箱の銭四五文や夕時雨

jūbako no zeni shi go mon ya yū shigure

in the box
four or five pennies...
night of winter rain

This haiku has the headnote, "A temple courtyard beggar."
Issa recopies it in *Oraga haru* with the headnote, "Taking pity
on a beggar at Zenkō Temple's gate."

1821

しぐるるや芭蕉翁の塚まはり

shigururu ya bashō okina no tsuka mawari

winter rain—
around Bashō's grave
falling down

The great haiku poet Bashō was affectionately known as the
"Old Man" (*okina* 翁). Though Issa couldn't visit Bashō's
grave that year on Bashō's Death-Day (twelfth day of Tenth
Month), he wrote this haiku in his honor. Bashō's grave is at
Gichū Temple in Ōtsu, near Kyoto.

1821

古郷は小意地の悪い時雨哉

furusato wa ko iji no warui shigure kana

my home village
in an ugly mood...
the winter rain

1823

いざこざを雀もいふや村しぐれ

izakoza wo suzume mo iu ya mura shigure

even the sparrows
are quarreling—
steady winter rain

1824

庵迄送りとどけて行時雨

iori made okuri-todokete yuku shigure

seeing me home
to my hut...
the winter rain

year unknown

かけがねの真赤に錆びて時雨哉

kake-gane no makka ni sabite shigure kana

the door latch
rusting scarlet...
winter rain

year unknown

しぐるるや逃る足さへちんば鶏

shigururu ya nigeru ashi sae chinba-dori

winter rain—
the lame chicken
limps away

1824

寒空のどこでとしよる旅乞食

samu-zora no doko de toshiyoru tabi kojiki

cold winter sky—
where will this wandering beggar
grow old?

1804

木がらしに三尺店も我夜也

kogarashi ni san-jakudana mo waga yo nari

in winter wind
in three-foot wide lodgings...
my night

1807

木がらしにくすくす豚の寝たりけり

kogarashi ni kusu-kusu buta no netari keri

in winter wind
the pig giggles
in his sleep

1811

木がらしにしくしく腹のぐあい哉

kogarashi ni shiku-shiku hara no guai kana

in winter wind
a churning, churning
in my belly

1816

木がらしや餌蒔の跡をおふ鳥
kogarashi ya emaki no ato wo ou karasu

winter wind—
behind the farmer sowing seeds
a crow

1819

木がらしや二十四文の遊女小家
kogarashi ya ni jū shi mon no yūjo-goya

winter wind—
a twenty-four penny
whorehouse

Charging just 24 *mon*, the price of about four bowls of rice in Issa's day, the women in the little shack are the lowest grade of prostitute. Issa conveys his deep sympathy for them by his apt juxtaposition of their hovel and the winter wind.

1824

木がらしに鼾盛りの屑家哉
kogarashi ni ibiki-zakari no kuzuya kana

winter wind—
a crescendo of snores
in my trashy house

405

1824

木がらしの掃てくれけり門の芥

kogarashi no haite kure keri kado no gomi

kindly the winter wind
sweeps
my gate

1806

初霜や茎の歯ぎれも去年迄

hatsu shimo ya kuki no hagire mo kyonen made

first frost—
my teeth could crack radishes
up to last year

A poem about aging. Jean Cholley notes that this haiku is one of many that laments Issa's loss of his teeth as he grew older; *En village de miséreux* 236-37. Literally, he misses cracking "stems" (*kuki* 茎): root vegetables like radishes.

1815

初霜や笑顔見せたる茶の聖

hatsu shimo ya egao misetaru cha no hijiri

first frost—
the smiling face
of the tea master

1794

朝霜に野鍛冶が散火走る哉
asa-jimo ni no kaji ga chiribi hashiru kana

on the morning frost
the blacksmith's sparks
spurting

1819

さをしかやえひしてなめるけさの霜
saoshika ya eishite nameru kesa no shimo

young bucks
licking each other...
morning frost

The editors of *Issa zenshū* picture the bucks licking the morning frost off each other (6.174).

1820

乞食子や膝の上迄けさの霜
kojiki ko ya hiza no ue made kesa no shimo

beggar child—
even in his lap
morning frost

Or "her lap."

1823

霜の夜や窓かいて鳴く勘当猫

shimo no yo ya mado kaite naku kandō neko

frosty night—
scratching the window, crying
banished cat

1824

霜の夜や七貧人の小寄合

shimo no yo ya shichi hinjin no ko yoriai

frosty night—
seven poor men
in a huddle

1803

初雪のふはふはかかる小鬢哉

hatsu yuki no fuwa-fuwa kakaru kobin kana

the first snow
softly, softly clings...
side lock of hair

1810

はつ雪が降とや腹の虫が鳴
hatsu yuki ga furu to ya hara no mushi ga naku

first snowfall—
the worms in my belly
sing

1810

はつ雪や朝夷する門乞食
hatsu yuki ya asaebisu suru kado kojiki

first snowfall—
early morning at my gate
a beggar

Or: "at the gate." Issa doesn't identify the gate as his, but this seems to be his meaning.

1810

はつ雪や雪やといふも歯なし哉
hatsu yuki ya yuki ya to iu mo ha nashi kana

"First snowfall, snowfall!"
he says
without teeth

Or: "I say"; Issa doesn't specify who is speaking.

1812

はつ雪や犬が先ふむ二文橋
hatsu yuki ya inu ga mazu fumu ni mon-bashi

in first snow
the dog goes first...
two-penny bridge

1814

はつ雪やどなたが這入る野雪隠
hatsu yuki ya donata ga hairu no setchin

first snowfall—
someone has entered
the outhouse

1817

はつ雪や机の上に一握り
hatsu yuki ya tsukue no ue ni hito nigiri

first snow—
on the desktop
a snowball

1818

闇夜のはつ雪らしやぼんの凹
yami no yo no hatsu yuki rashi ya bon no kubo

dark night—
the first snowflakes
hit my neck

1819

初雪や今に煮らるる豚あそぶ
hatsu yuki ya ima ni niraruru buta asobu

first snowfall—
soon to be boiled
the playful pig

1822

はつ雪や御きげんのよい御烏
hatsu yuki ya o-kigen no yoi on-garasu

first snowfall—
in a splendid mood
Sir Crow

1824

はつ雪や降りもかくれぬ犬の糞
hatsu yuki ya furi ni mo kakurenu inu no kuso

the first snowfall
doesn't hide it...
dog poop

1790

山寺や雪の底なる鐘の声
yamadera ya yuki no soko naru kane no koe

mountain temple—
deep under snow
a bell

year unknown

じつとして雪をふらすや牧の駒
jitto shite yuki wo furasu ya maki no koma

stone still
he lets the snow fall
colt in the pasture

1805

只居ればおるとて雪の降にけり

tada oreba oru tote yuki no furi ni keri

just existing
I exist...
snow flitting down

1805

夜の雪だまつて通る人もあり

yoru no yuki damatte tōru hito mo ari

night snow—
in a hush people
passing

1812

是がまあつひの栖か雪五尺

kore ga maa tsui no sumika ka yuki go shaku

well here it is,
the place I'll die?
five feet of snow

Viewed by many as his death verse, this haiku was etched on Issa's gravestone. He wrote it some time after the 24th day of Eleventh Month, 1812, when he returned to his native village, determined to fulfill his father's dying wish for him to live in the family home. By Second Month of 1813, his inheritance dispute with his stepmother was resolved, and he returned for good. In March 2015 while visiting Issa's home province of Nagano, I and Issa scholar Tsukasa Tamaki viewed the original manuscript in which this haiku appears: a small notebook filled with Issa's haiku in black with corrections in red by his haiku teacher and benefactor Natusme Seibi. To the side of the middle phrase, *tsui no sumika ka* つひの栖か ("my last residence?"), Issa offered an alternative middle phrase, which Seibi rejected by crossing it out. Professor Tamaki translates Issa's alternative version as "my death place?" We agreed that Seibi was wrong to reject this much stronger statement. I've emended my translation to reflect Issa's alternate version.

1812
掌へはらはら雪の降りにけり
tenohira e hara-hara yuki no furi ni keri

to my open palms
snowflakes flitting
down

1813

むまさうな雪がふうはりふはり哉

mumasōna yuki ga fūwari fuwari kana

looking delicious
the snow flitting softly
softly

1813

大雪や印の竿を鳴く烏

ōyuki ya shirushi no sao wo naku karasu

deep snow—
on the signpost
a crow caws

1820

重荷負ふ牛や頭につもる雪

omoni ou ushi ya atama ni tsumoru yuki

it's a load
on the cow's head...
pile of snow

1820

真直な小便穴や門の雪

massuguna shōben ana ya kado no yuki

what a straight
piss hole!
snow at the gate

1822

子どもらが雪喰ながら湯治かな

kodomora ga yuki kui nagara tōji kana

children eat snow
soaking
in the hot spring

1823

雪ちるや雪駄の音のさわがしき

yuki chiru ya setta no oto no sawagashiki

falling snow—
the sound of snowshoes
chomp! chomp!

1825

隣から連小便や夜の雪
tonari kara tsure shōben ya yoru no yuki

pissing
with the neighbor...
evening snow

1825

雪の日や堂にぎつしり鳩雀
yuki no hi ya dō ni gisshiri hato suzume

on a snowy day
the temple is packed...
pigeons, sparrows

1827

降る雪を払ふ気もなきかがし哉
furu yuki wo harau ki mo naki kagashi kana

he's also in no mood
to sweep the snow...
scarecrow

1794

灯ちらちら疱瘡小家の吹雪哉
hi chira-chira mogasa ko ie no fubuki kana

lamplight flickers
in the smallpox shack...
a blizzard

1820

さ筵や猫がきて来た太平雪
samushiro ya neko ga kite kita tabira yuki

little straw mat—
the cat comes with a coat
of snowflakes

1813

霰来とうたへる口へあられ哉
arare ku to utaeru kuchi e arare kana

into the mouth singing
"Come, hailstones!"
a hailstone

1813

霰ちれくくり枕を負ふ子ども
arare chire kukurimakura wo ou kodomo

fall, hailstones!
with pillow on his head
a child

1813

玉霰それそれ兄が耳房に
tama arare sore sore ani ga mimi fusa ni

hailstones—
look! there's one behind
brother's ear

1813

ちりめんの猿を抱く子よ丸雪ちる
chirimen no saru wo daku ko yo arare chiru

the child hugs
her cloth monkey...
hailstorm

Or: "his cloth monkey."

419

1814

ちる霰立小便の見事さよ

chiru arare tachi shōben no migotosa yo

to stand pissing
while hailstones fall...
quite a feat!

1815

明神にほうり出された霰哉

myōjin ni hōridasareta arare kana

let loose
by some god above...
hailstones

1818

懐に袂に霰々哉

futokoro ni tamoto ni arare arare kana

in the pockets
in the sleeves...
hailstones!

1821

三絃のばちで掃きやる霰哉
samisen no bachi de haki yaru arare kana

with the samisen's
plectrum sweeping up...
hailstones

A samisen is a long-necked, three-stringed banjo-like instrument, plucked with a plectrum. Here, someone is finding a new use for the latter. By implication, a geisha or courtesan is performing the action. The setting may be Yoshiwara, the licensed brothel district near Edo.

year unknown
念仏に拍子付たる霰哉
nembutsu ni hyōshi tsuketaru arare kana

keeping the beat
of the prayer to Buddha...
hailstones

The prayer being chanted is the *nembutsu.* "Namu Amida Butsu" ("All praise to Amida Buddha!").

1803

酒菰の戸口明りやみぞれふる
sakagomo no toguchi akari ya mizore furu

my sake keg
open for business...
sleet pours down

1793

遠方や枯野の小家の灯の見ゆる
enpō ya kareno no-goya no hi no miyuru

distant sight—
in withered fields
a little house's lamp

1814

御談義の手まねも見ゆるかれの哉
o-dangi no temane mo miyuru kareno kana

the preacher's
hand gestures too...
withered fields

1819

西方は極楽道よかれのはら

saihō wa gokuraku michi yo kareno hara

to the west
is Buddha's Paradise...
withered fields

The withered fields symbolize the passing of life—and the need to trust in Amida Buddha's "Other Power" to be reborn in the Pure Land, a metaphor for enlightenment. The fields being withered suggest our own bodies' rapid withering, as Issa's thoughts bend toward death. According to Buddhist myth paradise lies somewhere to the west.

1824

吹風に声も枯野の烏かな

fuku kaze ni koe mo kareno no karasu kana

voices in the wind
the withered field's
crows

Or: "a voice...a crow."

1806

もろもろの愚者も月見る十夜哉

moro-moro no gusha mo tsuki miru jūya kana

all sorts of fools
moon-gaze too...
winter prayers

"Winter prayers" refer to the Ten Nights Festival, a Tenth Month event during which people gathered at Pure Land temples to recite the *nembutsu*.

1819

御十夜は巾着切も月夜也

o-jūya wa kinchakukiri mo tsuki yo nari

winter prayers—
a cutpurse, too
in moonlight

1819

菜畠を通してくれる十夜哉

na-batake wo tōshite kureru jūya kana

he lets me cross
his field...
night of winter prayers

1825

庵の犬送つてくれる叙骸ニ

io no inu okutte kureru jūya kana

the hut's dog is escort
to the winter
prayers

1807

我塚もやがて頼むぞ鉢敲

waga tsuka mo yagate tanomu zo hachi tataki

my grave too
will soon need his prayer...
a monk beats his bowl

Beginning with the thirteenth day of Eleventh Month and continuing for 48 days thereafter, certain Buddhist priests went on pilgrimage each night, reciting the *nembu-tsu* and singing religious songs. Since they had to beg for food along the way, they announced their presence and need by banging on their bowls.

1822

つぐらから猫が面出すいろり哉

tsugura kara neko ga tsura dasu irori kana

from a straw basket
the cat's face...
by the hearth

1812

かくれ家や犬の天窓のすすもはく

kakurega ya inu no atama no susu mo haku

secluded house—
sweeping soot
off the dog's head, too

1817

庵の煤掃く真似をして置にけり

io no susu haku mane wo shite oki ni keri

my hut's soot—
going through the motions
of sweeping it

1820

庵の煤風が払つてくれにけり

io no susu kaze ga haratte kure ni keri

kindly the wind

sweeps my sooty

hut

1821

隅の蜘案じな煤はとらぬぞよ

sumi no kumo anjina susu wa toranu zo yo

corner spider

rest easy, my soot-broom

is idle

1822

煤竹や仏の顔も一なぐり

susutake ya hotoke no kao mo hito naguri

bamboo soot-broom—

Buddha's face too

gets a smack

Issa is referring to a statue of Buddha.

1819

犬の餅烏が餅もつかれけり
inu no mochi karasu ga mochi mo tsukare keri

one for the dog
one for the crow...
rice cakes

1820

かくれ家や猫が三疋もちのばん
kakurega ya neko ga sambiki mochi no ban

secluded house—
three cats guard
the rice cakes

1822

木がくれやとしとりもちもひとりつく
kogakure ya toshitori mochi mo hitori tsuku

tree shade—
an old man pounds rice cakes
alone

1819

古反故を継合せつつ羽織哉

furu hogo wo tsugi awase tsutsu haori kana

patched
with old wastepaper
my winter coat

1810

こほろぎの寒宿とする衾哉

kōrogi no kanshuku to suru fusuma kana

the cricket's
winter residence...
my quilt

year unknown

鼠らよ小便無用古衾

nezumi-ra yo shōben muyō furu fusuma

hey mice
no pissing on my old
winter quilt!

1815

屁くらべが已に始る衾かな

he kurabe ga sude ni hajimaru fusuma kana

the farting contest
begins at once...
winter quilt

1813

安房猫おのがふとんは知にけり

ahō neko ono ga futon wa shiri ni keri

fool cat—
yet he knows which futon
is his

1813

さる人が真丸に寝るふとん哉

saru hito ga manmaru ni neru futon kana

the man who left
slept in a ball...
futon

1821

寺道や老母を乗てそりを引
tera michi ya rōbo wo nosete sori wo hiku

temple road—
his aged mother rides
the snow sled

year unknown

そり引や犬が上荷乗て行
sori hiku ya inu ga uwani nosete yuku

a man pulls a snow sled
a dog atop
the cargo

1813

御ひざに雀鳴也雪仏
on-hiza ni suzume naku nari yuki-botoke

a sparrow chirping
in his lap...
snow Buddha

1813

とるとしもあなた任せぞ雪仏
torutoshi mo anata makase zo yuki-botoke

growing old too
I trust in a Buddha
of snow

1815

寄合つて雀がはやす雪仏
yoriatte suzume ga hayasu yuki-botoke

sparrows gather
and cheer...
my snow Buddha

1824

門先や雪の仏も苦い顔
kado saki ya yuki no hotoke mo nigai-gao

at my gate
the snow Buddha also
scowls

1793

冬篭り鳥料理にも念仏哉
fuyugomori tori ryōri ni mo nebutsu kana

winter seclusion—
cooking a chicken
praising Buddha

Once again Issa mentions the prayer to Amida Buddha
(shortening the pronunciation of *nembutsu* to *nebutsu* to fit
the ideal 5-7-5 pattern of sound units). Eons ago, Amida
promised that all who rely on his liberating power would be
reborn in the Pure Land (the Western Paradise). This means
that even a sinner who has killed a chicken, trusting in
Amida, can reach the Pure Land—both a mythic place and a
metaphor for enlightenment.

1803

御迎ひの鐘の鳴也冬篭
o-mukai no kane no naru nari fuyugomori

the death bell
tolls at the temple...
winter seclusion

1813

猪熊と隣づからや冬篭

shishi kuma to tonari-zukara ya fuyugomori

boars and bears
are my neighbors...
winter seclusion

1819

のふなしはつみも又なし冬ごもり

nō nashi wa tsumi mo mata nashi fuyugomori

no good deeds
but also no sins...
winter seclusion

1821

煩悩の犬もつきそふ冬篭

bonnō no inu mo tsukisō fuyugomori

my sinful dog
at my side...
winter seclusion

1822

人誹る会が立なり冬籠
hito soshiru kai ga tatsunari fuyugomori

the slander parties
begin...
winter seclusion

Villagers confined in their houses during the coldest months
had nothing better to do than to indulge in evil talk about
their neighbors; see Makoto Ueda, *Dew on the Grass* 151.

1824

こほろぎもついて来にけり冬篭り
kōrogi mo tsuite ki ni keri fuyugomori

the cricket also
moves in with me...
winter seclusion

1817

大名は濡れて通るを炬燵哉
daimyō wa nurete tōru wo kotatsu kana

a war lord
drenching wet, passes
my cozy brazier

A *kotatsu* 炬燵 is a quilt-covered brazier.

1813

一茶坊に過たるものや炭一俵
issa-bō ni sugitaru mono ya sumi ippyō

more than enough
for Priest Issa...
one bag of coal

1819

炭の火や旦の祝儀の咳ばらひ
sumi no hi ya asa no shūgi no sekibarai

charcoal fire—
morning's celebration
of coughing

1813

雲と見し桜は炭にやかれけり
kumo to mishi sakura wa sumi ni yakare keri

the cherry tree
that made blossom clouds
becomes charcoal

Charcoal is being made in a kiln. In this case, the wood is of a cherry tree.

1813

炭竈のちよぼちよぼけぶる長閑さよ
sumigama no chobo chobo keburu nodokasa yo

the charcoal kiln's smoke
puff by puff...
tranquility

1792

ほたの火や糸取窓の影ぼうし
hota no hi ya ito toru mado no kagebōshi

a wood fire—
her shadow in the window
pulling thread

The figure in the window is pulling thread from cotton—
"woman's work," according to Maruyama Kazuhiko; *Issa haiku shū* 一茶俳句集 19.

1819

大名の一番立のほた火哉

daimyō no ichiban-dachi no hotabi kana

the war lord's wood fire

rises

first

1811

埋火の芋をながむる烏哉

uzumibi no imo wo nagamuru karasu kana

eyeing the potato

on the banked fire…

crow

This haiku is a rewrite of one that Issa composed the year before. The revision substitutes "potato" for "rice cake." Interestingly, Issa didn't seem able to make up his mind on this poem; in the revision he writes "potato" (*imo* 芋) and "rice cake" (*mochi* 餅) side by side; *IZ* 2.586. A banked fire is a fire covered with ashes to ensure low burning.

1810

茎漬の氷こごりを歯切哉
kukizuke no kōri kogori wo hagiri kana

frozen pickle water—
my teeth
crackle

1822

蛇の鮨も喰かねぬ也薬なら
ja no sushi mo kuwa-kanenu nari kusuri nara

even snake sushi
is given a try...
winter medicine

"Medicine" (*kusuri* 薬) is a winter season word. As this haiku indicates, some unusual cures were tried.

1822

相ばんに猫も並ぶや薬喰
shōban ni neko mo narabu ya kusuri kuu

even the cat
lines up for his share...
taking medicine

1803

浅ましと鰒や見らん人の顔
asamashi to fugu ya miruran hito no kao

looking shameful
to the pufferfish...
people's faces

A humorous role-reversal. People may think that the fish has an ugly face, but, Issa imagines, this negative perception could go both ways. Pufferfish soup is a winter season word.

1814

胡坐して猿も座とるや鰒汁
agura shite saru mo za toru ya fukuto-jiru

sitting cross-legged
a monkey joins too...
pufferfish soup

1806

風吹や猪の寝顔の欲げなき
kaze fuku ya shishi no ne-gao no hoshige naki

wind blows—
the wild boar's sleeping face
so innocent

1824

木兎や上手に眠る竿の先
mimizuku ya jyōzu ni nemuru sao no saki

scops owl—
sleeping so well
atop the pole

1804

山風を踏こたへたりみそさざい
yama kaze wo fumi kotaetari misosazai

fighting the mountain wind
on foot...
a wren

1814

野はこせん見ることなかれみそさざい
no hako sen miru koto nakare misosazai

pooping in the field—
avert your eyes
little wren!

1822

うす壁や鼠穴よりみそさざい

usu kabe ya nezumi ana yori misosazai

thin wall—
from the mouse's hole
a wren!

1810

小夜千鳥人は三十日を鳴にけり

sayo chidori hito wa misoka wo naki ni keri

evening plovers—
bills are due
people are crying

Shinji Ogawa explains that the plovers are crying for one reason and people for another: "People must pay their debts at the end of the month." I decided to use Shinji's insight in my translation. However, a more literal translation would be: "evening plovers—/ at the end of the month/ people are crying."

1824

声々や子どもの交じる浜千鳥
koe-goe ya kodomo no majiru hama chidori

an uproar on the beach—
children
and plovers

1811

冬の蝿逃せば猫にとられけり
fuyu no hae nigaseba neko ni torare keri

the winter fly
I spare, the cat
snatches

1820

たがたがと枯恥かくな乱れ菊
taga-taga to kare haji kaku na midare-giku

there's no shame
that you totter...
old chrysanthemum

Or: "chrysanthemums." It is winter and the flower totters, but Issa sees no shame in this. It has survived a long time, outliving other flowers. The chrysanthemum is a role model.

1819

六道の辻に立けりかれ尾花
roku dō no tsuji ni tachi keri kare obana

standing at a six-way
crossroads...
withered grasses

This haiku alludes to the "Six Ways" of Buddhist reincarnation: (1) as a sufferer in hell, (2) as a hungry ghost, (3) as an animal, (4) as an angry demon, (5) as a human being, or (6) as a heavenly being.

1803

大根引一本づつに雲を見る
daikon hiku ippon-zutsu ni kumo wo miru

yanking radishes
one by one...
watching the clouds

Although many English-speaking readers these days know what a *daikon* 大根 is, I continue to translate it with the more familiar (though technically inaccurate) term, "radish."

1814

大根引大根で道を教へけり
daiko hiki daiko de michi wo oshie keri

with a just-yanked
radish
pointing the way

In this haiku and the third one following it (see below), *daikon* 大根 is read *daiko* to preserve the 5-7-5 pattern of sound units.

1817

大根で叩きあふたる子ども哉
daikon de tataki autaru kodomo kana

a battle royal
with radishes...
children

1819

尼達や二人かかつて引大根
ama-dachi ya futatsu kakatte hiki daikon

temple nuns—
it takes two
yanking the radish

1819

大根引拍子にころり小僧哉

daiko hiku hyōshi ni korori kozō kana

yanking a radish
taking a tumble...
little boy

1825

大根で鹿追まくる畠哉

daikon de shika oimakuru hatake kana

with a radish
driving off a deer...
his field

Or: "her field."

1818

あにかれじかれじと見しは欲目也

ani kareji kareji to mishi wa yokume nari

my thought
the tree would never wither
was wrong

The meaning of this rather obscure haiku is clarified by
the one that immediately precedes it in Issa's journal

Shichiban nikki: ima mireba mina yokume nari kareta ume 今見れば皆欲目也枯れた梅 ("remembering how it was/ with yearning.../ bare winter plum"). Shinji Ogawa paraphrases it: "having thought 'It won't wither! It won't wither!' turned out to be a partial view" ("partial" in the sense of "biased"). Issa wanted to believe his tree would stay lush and green forever.

1820

猫の子のちよいと押へる木の葉かな
neko no ko no choi to osaeru konoha kana

the kitten holds it down
just a moment...
fallen leaf

1814

藪並におれが首も枯にけり
yabu nami ni ore ga kōbe mo kare ni keri

stand of trees—
my head too
withered and bare

1806

帰り咲分別もない垣ね哉
kaeri-zaku funbetsu mo nai kakine kana

lacking good sense
out-of-season flowers
on the fence

"Out-of-season blooming" (*kaeri-zaku* 帰り咲) is a winter seasonal expression. Here, the premature blooms indicate, to Issa, a lack of discretion; winter is not over.

1819

一人の太平楽や年わすれ
ichi nin no taiheiraku ya toshiwasure

all alone
babbling idiocies...
drinking away the year

This haiku and the following three refer to an end-of-year drinking party.

1819

御仲間に猫も坐とるや年わすれ

o-nakama ni neko mo za toru ya toshiwasure

the cat joins
the party...
drinking away the year

1819

都哉橋の下にも年わすれ

miyako kana hashi no shita ni mo toshiwasure

Kyoto—
even under bridges
drinking away the year

1824

一人居や一徳利のとし忘

hitori i ya hito tokkuri no toshiwasure

living alone—
just one bottle
for drinking away the year

1819

ともかくもあなた任せのとしの暮

tomokaku mo anata makase no toshi no kure

come what may
trusting in the Buddha
the year ends

This is the closing haiku in Issa's 1819 poetic journal, *Oraga haru*. At the end of a difficult year during which he lost his precious daughter Sato, the poet places his trust, utterly, in Amida Buddha.

1823

風鈴やちんぷんかんのとしの暮れ

fūrin ya chinpunkan no toshi no kure

a wind-chime's
empty babble ends
the year

9. HAIKU WITHOUT SEASON WORDS

1811

月花や四十九年のむだ歩き
tsuki hana ya shi jūku nen no muda aruki

moon! blossoms!
forty-nine years walking around
a waste

This haiku is one of mixed seasons: "moon" suggests autumn (the harvest moon), and "blossoms" suggest spring. The opening phrase evokes Issa's haiku journey through life.

1812

五寸釘松もほろほろ涙哉
go sun kugi matsu mo horo-horo namida kana

a five-inch nail—
the pine tree
is weeping

1812

仏ともならでうかうか老の松
hotoke tomo narade uka-uka oi no matsu

not yet Buddha—
the mindless old
pine

Uka-uka うかうか is an old expression meaning (1) not at peace or (2) thoughtless or absentminded; *KDJ* 182. In my translation, I have chosen the second meaning. With its non-thinking, non-mindedness the pine is well on the way to achieving enlightenment. However, the first meaning might also apply, taking the haiku in a completely different direction. Agitated by the wind perhaps, the pine doesn't show the perfect calm of the Buddha that it will one day become.

1812

からからと音して亀を引ずりぬ
kara-kara to oto shite kame wo hikizurinu

with a thump, thump
the turtle drags
along

1809

此次は我身の上かなく烏

kono tsugi wa waga mi no ue ka naku karasu

will I be the next one
you caw over?
crows

This haiku has a headnote: "Elegy for Master Kōshun." According to Jean Cholley, the deceased, Kōshun (Tokizawa Yūzō), was Issa's friend; *En village de miséreux* 237.

1818

士の供を連たる御犬哉

samurai no tomo wo tsuretaru o-inu kana

joining the samurai's
company...
Sir Dog

1812

のら猫が仏のひざを枕哉

nora neko ga hotoke no hiza wo makura kana

the stray cat
makes Buddha's lap
her pillow

Or: "his pillow."

1812

亡母や海見る度に見る度に

naki haha ya umi miru tabi ni miru tabi ni

my dead mother—
every time I see the ocean
every time...

1817

君なくて誠に多太の木立哉

kimi nakute makoto ni tada no kodachi kana

without you—
the grove
is just a grove

ABOUT THE TRANSLATOR

David G. Lanoue is a professor of English at Xavier University of Louisiana. He is a cofounder of the New Orleans Haiku Society, an associate member of the Haiku Foundation, and former President of the Haiku Society of America. His books include translations (*Cup-of-Tea Poems* and *Issa's Best*), criticism (*Pure Land Haiku, Issa and the Meaning of Animals,* and *Issa and Being Human*), haiku collections (*On a Sign Pointing Two Ways* and *A Feeling of Curiosity*), a how-to book (*Write like Issa*), a series of "haiku novels," including *Haiku Guy, Laughing Buddha, Haiku Wars, Frog Poet,* and *Dewdrop World,* and a book-length *haibun, My Journal with Haiku Spinkled in,* written to celebrate the 200th anniversary of Issa's *Oraga Haru.* Some of his books have appeared in French, German, Spanish, Bulgarian, Serbian, and Japanese editions. He maintains *The Haiku of Kobayashi Issa* website, for which he translated 10,000 of Issa's haiku.

Printed in Dunstable, United Kingdom